Praise for *Praying Thro...*

"What an encouraging devotional! Written by women who have walked the road and speak from experience, it demonstrates how God can enable you to come through the trials of cancer with praise on your lips, peace in your spirit, and hope in your heart."

—Kay Marshall Strom, author of *The Cancer Survival Guide*

"For the past twenty-five years it has been my privilege to participate in the care of patients battling cancer. This poignant collection of "been there done that" provides a practical spiritual framework for patients, physicians, nurses, friends, and pastors (i.e. the team) to laugh, cry, and encourage one another. Most importantly it keeps our eyes upon Him. Our God is an awesome God!"

—Dr. Steven Andresen, Cleveland Clinic

"*Praying Through Cancer* offers great wisdom through very faithful witnesses. Along with practical advice, it offers biblical insights that lift the spirit and encourage the soul. I heartily recommend this book to you."

—Rev. Dr. Michael Barry, Director of Pastoral Care at the Cancer Treatment Centers of America at Eastern Regional Medical Center, Philadelphia, PA; Author of *A Reason For Hope, Finding Strength for Your Fight Against Cancer*

"Journeying through breast cancer, the most authentic voices that encouraged me were women who have pilgrimmed ahead of me. *Praying through Cancer* is rich and real, each page speaking to all the questions and fears that accompany such a diagnosis. This book nourished my spirit and renewed my hope—may it do the same for you."

—Karen Hill

Author of *Owen's Walk* and Assistant to Max Lucado

"Often hairless and prayerless, we stumble forward on the cancer journey. But these sisters wait with outstretched hands to lead us into the open arms of our heavenly Father. Each day in this wonderful little book there's a reminder that we were created to soar, no matter what."

—Judy Asti

Author of *A Spiritual Journey Through Breast Cancer*

"I highly recommend this devotional book to accompany the time you spend in God's Word if you (or a loved one) are going through a cancer journey! You will be encouraged and challenged as you go through this season of life! I wish this book would have been available to my wife, as primary caregiver, and I when we went through my journey. A special thanks to Susan, Laura and others for sharing their lives with us!"

—Kevin Winningham,
LifeStage Ministries Pastor
NorthRidge Church
Plymouth, Michigan

Praying Through
CANCER

Set Your Heart Free from Fear

A 90-DAY DEVOTIONAL *for* WOMEN

Susan Sorensen & Laura Geist

THOMAS NELSON
Since 1798

NASHVILLE   DALLAS   MEXICO CITY   RIO DE JANEIRO

PRAYING THROUGH CANCER

© 2006 Susan Sorensen and Laura Geist.

Published in Nashville, Tennessee. Thomas Nelson is a registered trademark of Thomas Nelson, Inc.

Thomas Nelson, Inc. titles may be purchased in bulk for educational, business, fundraising, or sales promotional use. For information, please email SpecialMarkets@ThomasNelson.com.

All Scripture quotations, unless otherwise indicated, are taken from The Holy Bible, New International Version®. Copyright © 1973, 1978, 1984 by International Bible Society. Used by permission of Zondervan. All rights reserved.

Other Scripture quotations are taken from the following sources: Used by permission of NavPress Publishing Group. All rights reserved. The American Standard Version (ASV). Public domain. The King James Version (KJV). The Message (MSG) by Eugene H. Peterson. Copyright © 1993, 1994, 1995, 1996, 2000, 2001, 2002. The New American Standard Version (NASB). Copyright © 1960, 1962, 1963, 1968, 1971, 1972, 1973, 1975, 1977, 1995 by The Lockman Foundation. Used by permission. The New Century Version® (NCV®). Copyright © 1987, 1988, 1991 by Thomas Nelson, Inc. Used by permission. All rights reserved. The New Jerusalem Bible (NJB). Copyright © 1985 by Darton, Longman & Todd Ltd. and Doubleday, a division of Random House, Inc. All rights reserved. The New King James Version (NKJV®), copyright 1979, 1980, 1982, Thomas Nelson, Inc., Publishers. The Holy Bible, New Living Translation® (NLT). Copyright © 1996. Used by permission of Tyndale House Publishers, Inc., Wheaton, IL 60189. All rights reserved. The New Revised Standard Version Bible (NRSV), © 1989 by the Division of Christian Education of the National Council of the Churches of Christ in the United States of America. Used by permission. All rights reserved. The Holy Bible: Revised Standard Version (RSV). Copyright © 1946, 1952, 1973 by National Council of Churches of Christ. All rights reserved. The Living Bible (TLB). Copyright © 1971 by Tyndale House Publishers, Inc. Used by permission. All rights reserved.

Cover Design: Designpoint, Inc.
Interior Design: Mandi Cofer

Library of Congress Cataloging-in-Publication Data

Praying through cancer : set your heart free from fear : a 90 day devotional for women / [compiled] by Susan Sorensen & Laura Geist.

    p. cm.
    Includes bibliographical references and index.
    ISBN 10: 0-8499-1882-0 (trade paper)
    ISBN 13: 978-0-8499-1882-7 (trade paper)
    ISBN 10: 0-8499-0021-2 (hardcover)
    ISBN 13: 978-0-8499-0021-1 (hardcover)

    1. Cancer in women—Prayer-books and devotions—English. 2. Cancer—Patients—Prayer-books and devotions—English. 3. Christian women—Prayer-books and devotions—English. I. Sorensen, Susan. II. Geist, Laura.
  BV4910.33.P73 2006
  242'.4--dc22
  2005022146

Printed in the United States of America
17 RRD 30

To Scott and Gordy—

You have undergirded us with heaven-sent strength
and wisdom. Thank you for being wonderful partners
through the joys and trials we have faced.

Contents

Contents

Contents

Contents

Acknowledgments

Susan Sorensen—To my husband, Scott, who loved me through follow-up visits from thyroid cancer the first years of our marriage and then traveled the new road of breast cancer these later years. You have been a rock as you have been the leader of our home, pointing us to Christ. You have often said that though circumstances are crashing around us, our Lord is unmoving and unchanging in His love. Thank you for those reminders.

To our children, Stephen and Sean, who though young have learned from this journey that has brought us closer to each other and closer to our Lord.

To my parents, John and Linda McDonald, who have been such a support since I found out I had cancer at nineteen. Thank you for your love and encouragement during all I've been through.

To two amazing medical institutions at which I was privileged to be treated—MD Anderson in Houston, Texas, and the Cleveland Clinic—thank you to all my doctors, nurses, and staff. Thanks to all my friends and family in Texas, Ohio, Michigan, New Mexico, Kansas, Arizona, and around the world who have faithfully supported and prayed for me throughout my life.

Laura Geist—To my husband, Gordy, who has traveled this

difficult journey with me and, with God's help, has been my constant source of strength and wisdom. We have been through so much together, and I can never imagine going through it without your amazing love. Thank you for challenging me to live radically for Christ so early in our relationship.

To my son, Geoff: You are a caring young man with a big heart for loving and serving others. Thanks for your big hugs and concern for me. To my daughter, Gretchen: Our relationship means the world to me. I love how God has matured you into a wonderful Christian young lady through adversity. Thanks for those special prayers!

To my mother, Laura Mai Clark, and my late father, Arthur Clark: Thank you for raising me to love Christ and encouraging me to use my writing ability.

To my three sisters, Janice Korstange, Marjorie Duncan, and Jennifer Condreay, who encouraged me to live not as a little sister but as a woman with purpose and strength!

To the many wonderful people at Highland Park Baptist Church, Southfield, Michigan, who ministered to me and loved me through it all.

To my medical team—Dr. Henry Maicki, Dr. Pamela Benitez, Dr. David Decker, Dr. Daniel Sherbert, and Dr. Larry Kestin—whose wisdom and talent in medicine made this journey easier. To all the caring employees at William Beaumont Hospital, Royal Oak, Michigan, who were instruments in my healing process. To my many friends and family who walked this difficult road with me and sometimes carried me on their backs! I love you and will never forget your kindness and self-lessness in my times of need.

From both of us—We both would like to acknowledge several individuals whose talents and vision made this book a reality.

Many thanks to Ruth and Warren Myers, whose book *31 Days of Praise* inspired this book and was a tremendous blessing to us.

To Debbie Petersen of the Women of Faith Conference: Thank you for introducing us to Thomas Nelson and for agreeing to be part of our project.

To Debbie Wickwire, acquisitions editor at Thomas Nelson: Thank you for believing in this unique project and catching a vision for ministering to women who have experienced cancer. Working with you has been a blessing.

To Laura Kendall and Adria Haley, our managing editors at Thomas Nelson: Thank you for putting the many pieces of this book together and for shepherding this project to completion.

To our photographer, Jeff Dykehouse, Dykehouse Photography, Grand Rapids, Michigan: Thanks for lending your wonderful talents to this project and inspiring us with your dedication to terminally ill children.

To our contributors: Thank you for sharing your stories so that others may know the Savior's love during cancer.

We're Praying
Through with You

We know the journey you are on, and we want to encourage you. When you hear the doctor say the word *cancer*, the fears can be overwhelming. Thankfully, there is a place of peace we found that we want you to experience. Through these pages, we desire to join you in this challenging time . . . to pray through cancer with you and to walk with you through it. Our greatest desire is that the testimonies and prayers in this book will strengthen and bless you in the months ahead.

FREE FROM FEAR

We will always remember the days leading up to our diagnoses of breast cancer. The process was very similar for us, even though we were diagnosed six months and hundreds of miles apart. You now know the routine. Your doctor sees a lump, shadow, or abnormality. He or she calls for some additional tests. Then you wait for the results. Days pass like weeks. Your emotions begin to overwhelm you. Then the phone call comes that confirms your worst fear: "It's malignant."

In a single moment, everything changes. You are shocked and bewildered. How could this happen? Fearful thoughts crash down like a flood. *How can I deal with the pain, the inconvenience, and the unknowns?*

We've been there. We will likely revisit fearful thoughts in the future. But there is hope even in the most difficult times. God does not want us to be overwhelmed by fear. He says, "Do not worry about anything, but pray and ask God for everything you need, always giving thanks" (Philippians 4:6 NCV). When we begin to worry, we have the incredible privilege of telling God about it and asking Him to provide all that we need.

The God of the universe wants you to "Cast all your anxiety on him because he cares for you" (1 Peter 5:7). The Greek word translated "cast" in this verse indicates the idea of throwing upon. Sometimes we can't gently give God our requests; we throw them at Him! Honestly, we've been there, especially in great disappointment. Thankfully, our Lord wants us to come and cast our cares on Him.

You Won't Be Alone

Life is a lot like driving down a two-lane country road with a huge eighteen-wheeler in front of you. You can't see around it. You can't get around it. Your every attempt to pass has been met by oncoming cars, which makes you even more fearful you will never move on.

But what if there was a helicopter above you with someone who loves you at the controls? Better yet, what if you could communicate with the person in the helicopter? That is what God has already done for us! He is in the helicopter. He can see what is in front of the truck and what is around the next bend. He can see the whole future clearly. As we communicate with Him, we can easily navigate around that big truck and move on to the next obstacle in the road.

While the analogy is somewhat simplistic, it is a reminder that we are dependent on God to help and navigate us through life. He wants to come alongside us and walk with us through our ups and downs.

THE GIFT OF HIS PRESENCE

One of God's greatest gifts is His presence. Our loving heavenly Father tells us to come to Him at any time, in any place, and with any emotion. God describes Himself in many powerful ways in the Bible. He is called the Rock, our Stronghold, a Tower, and our Refuge. We have the privilege of joining Him in this solid place. Though our circumstances may be swirling around us, we are able to join Him in a place of perfect security.

Are you struggling with trusting Him completely? We'd

encourage you to enter your Refuge and talk to God about everything on your heart—right now. Be honest with God.

THE GIFT OF HIS PEACE

God promises that when we pray about all that makes us anxious, He will give us peace. This is hard to imagine until we experience it.

We have the privilege of being married to men who know the power of prayer. The evenings following our diagnosis, we prayed with them. We asked God for healing, but we also asked Him for the strength to walk through this with His peace and provision. Each time we prayed together in the months that followed, we found that we walked away expectant, almost excited to see how God would work. We were filled with peace when the challenges of life should have prevented it.

FROM OUR HEARTS TO YOURS

The following devotionals and prayers were written out of personal experiences with cancer. The women who contributed share their stories of struggle and triumph in the face of uncertainty. They have one thing in common: they each experienced God's peace as they looked to our Lord and Savior. We know many of you will go through at least three months of treatment. The following ninety days of devotionals are designed with that in mind.

We pray that God will fill you with unexplainable peace as you look to the One who created you and loves you and will walk with you all of your days!

—Susan Sorensen and Laura Geist

Refined in the Fire

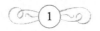

*But he knows the way that I take; when he
has tested me, I will come forth as gold.*

—JOB 23:10

The doctor was very matter-of-fact. When he told me I had
breast cancer, his inflection didn't change, his manner didn't
warm up, and he offered nothing in the way of comfort. He
left the room, leaving me to weep alone.

While this earthly man had no reaction to my diagnosis, my
heavenly Father *instantly* offered me His words of comfort and
peace. A Scripture fragment floated into my mind: "He knows
the way I take." In my shock and dismay, I couldn't remember
where it was from, but it gave me a lifeline to grab on to.

God, the Creator of the universe, the Almighty One, the
Lord of heaven and earth, *knew* the "way"—the journey I was
starting on. That meant He wasn't surprised (although I
certainly was) and had already begun to prepare all that I
would need along the way. My loving, purposeful Father had
factored cancer into His plan for me long before I was aware
of it. His eyes were on me; He held me in His tender gaze. I
wasn't alone anymore!

God, how can I ever thank You for showing up when I need You the most? I am never alone! You promise to be my refuge and my strength, my ever-present help in trouble. You are with me when I receive exciting, thrilling news, and You are with me even when I hear news that threatens to shake me to my core. Those dreaded words, "It's cancer," don't send You running from the room. Instead, You rush to bring me the assurance that You know exactly where I am.

There is nothing ahead of me that can detour Your will for my life. You will fulfill Your purpose for me. How I praise You for Your unfailing love. You are my God forever and ever, and You will be my guide even to the end. I trust You implicitly. May this furnace of testing show the true colors of my faith in You, and may I come forth as gold.

Kay Warren
Senior pastor's wife,
Saddleback Church

TODAY'S TIP: When you find yourself facing frightening moments, remind yourself that God stands with you. You are never alone!
PRAYER REFERENCES: Psalm 46:1; Psalm 138:8; Psalm 48: 9, 14; Job 23:10

Centered on Christ

Let us fix our eyes on Jesus,
the author and perfecter of our faith.
—Hebrews 12:2

I was riding an emotional roller coaster, and it wasn't pleasant. Every day, it seemed I would talk to someone else who had been through cancer. Some stories lifted my spirits. Others lowered me to despair. My ability to empathize is a bit too good. Emotionally, I was becoming the person I had talked with last!

I am learning to first fix my eyes on Jesus. Our unchanging Lord is the only stability in uncertain times. I love the story of Peter when he saw Jesus walking on the water. After Jesus bid him to come, "Peter got down out of the boat, walked on the water and came toward Jesus. But when he saw the wind, he was afraid and, beginning to sink, cried out, 'Lord, save me!'" (Matthew 14:29–30). I can just picture Peter with his eyes on Jesus, not even aware he is actually walking on water! Then he looks down, and fear grips him.

I have often joined Peter in crying out, "Lord, save me!" More times than I can count, Jesus has gently lifted my chin and helped me fix my eyes back on Him.

Lord, You are the author of my faith . . . the One who initiated my relationship with You, the One who chose me. You are also the perfecter of my faith. How grateful I am for the confidence I can have that You began a good work in me and that You will carry it on to completion until the day of Christ Jesus. I praise You for Your promise to rescue and protect me. You will be with me in times of trouble and deliver me and honor me. You will be with me forever.

Help me throw off everything that hinders me from complete trust in You. I want to run with perseverance the race marked out for me. For my sake, You endured the cross and sat down at the right hand of the throne of God. That You would do all this for me is beyond amazing. I praise Your holy name!

Susan Sorensen

TODAY'S TIP: Take a moment to walk on the water as you read Psalm 91.

PRAYER REFERENCES: Hebrews 12:2; Philippians 1:6; Psalm 91:14–16

An Unwelcome Intruder

*Everyone will know that the LORD
does not need weapons to rescue
his people. It is his battle, not ours.*
—1 SAMUEL 17:47 NLT

I've always felt I could ward off a lot of problems in life by anticipating them. You know, take an umbrella in case it rains. Always have restaurant coupons in the car in case I decide to go out to eat. Have an extra wrapped gift at Christmas in case I receive one I wasn't expecting. You get the idea.

Then *bam!* Cancer hit me from out of nowhere. I was young and healthy. I certainly hadn't anticipated this, and it was too late to get prepared now.

And then something else hit me.

This diagnosis did not take God by surprise. He saw it coming, and although I wish He had stopped it from touching me, He *was not* unprepared to battle it. In fact, He equipped me with everything I needed to fight physically, mentally, emotionally, and spiritually. Like the shepherd boy David going up against the nine-foot-tall Goliath, I knew my Lord had what it takes. With David I could say, "It is His battle, not mine."

Dear Lord, this cancer has taken me by surprise. I feel anxious, out of control, and woefully unprepared because I didn't see it coming. Yet I also know You are not surprised or anxious, and You are very much in control.

Help me put on Your armor each day: the belt of Your truth, the shield of Your righteousness, the shoes of Your peace, the helmet of Your salvation, and the sword of Your Spirit. Then I will be ready to battle this unwelcome intruder. And most of all, I will not be afraid because it really is Your battle. I trust You to fight in and through me so that I am not defeated by this unseen enemy.

Thank You, Holy Spirit, that I don't need to be in control to battle cancer—I just need to be controlled by You. Amen.

Lynn Eib
Author, *When God and Cancer Meet;*
Finding the Light in Cancer's Shadow

TODAY'S TIP: Read a psalm each morning, and you'll meet people disappointed by life yet still finding hope in God.

PRAYER REFERENCES: Ephesians 6:14–17;
1 Samuel 17:47

Throw Yourself a Party

Every good and perfect gift is from above,
coming down from the Father of the heavenly lights,
who does not change like shifting shadows.
—James 1:17

When I heard of my cancer diagnosis, I threw myself a party—a pity party! The first guest to arrive was Fear. In his gift, I found the fear of losing my friends and of facing financial pressure and my own mortality. Next to arrive was Doubt. Inside his gift was the doubt of whether I would see my children grow up and whether I would be attractive when this was over. Not far behind was Anger. His gift contained anger at how cancer would turn my life upside down, and yes, anger at God. Dread seemed to take his time getting to the party. His gift was the dread of the treatments and their side effects and the dread of losing my identity.

The last guest to arrive was Jesus. I raced toward Him and quickly opened His gift to discover:

Hope . . . promise for the future
Strength . . . the ability to endure

Grace . . . God's help
Comfort . . . in pain, trouble, and anxiety
Peace . . . calmness
Healing . . . restoration of mind, spirit, and body
Joy . . . a sense of well-being
Love . . . compassion and devotion shown by God

After opening all the presents, I realized that Jesus, with the beautiful gifts He freely gives, was the only One I needed or wanted to stay.

Most gracious heavenly Father, thank You for loving me enough to give me the most precious gift of all: Your Son, Jesus Christ. When I know Jesus, I am given the gift of Your Holy Spirit and a relationship that extends throughout eternity. Thank You for the promise that Your gifts and calling are irrevocable. I am Yours, and nothing can change that!

Forgive any fear, doubt, anger, and dread that I have as I come to grips with what lies before me. [Take a moment to share your specific concerns.] Bury deep within my heart the assurance that by Your grace I will be able to embrace my circumstances with peace and confidence.

I am grateful that You are able to make all grace abound to me so that in all things at all times I will have all that I need. Fill me up with all the gifts of Your Spirit: love, joy, peace, patience, kindness, goodness, faithfulness, and self-control. I praise You for the perfect gifts You give to Your children . . . that You have given to me.

Missy Morrow, mom
Ann Snuggs, interior/exterior designer

TODAY'S TIP: When you throw yourself a pity party—just remember to invite Jesus!

PRAYER REFERENCES: Romans 11:29; 2 Corinthians 9:8–11; Galatians 5:22–23; James 1:17

A Way in the Wilderness

I will not leave you desolate;
I will come to you.
—John 14:18 RSV

When I learned I had breast cancer, I was in the midst of studying about the people of Israel. God had a plan to bring them out of Egypt, but oh how they grumbled about where they ended up—in the wilderness. It seemed to me that if I rebelled against this bend in the road, I, like the Israelites, would be grumbling against God's goodness and purpose. So I determined to follow Him and trust His provision wherever He chose to lead me. He did provide for me there—the skillful surgeon, the many who prayed for me, the support of my family. It seemed like such a victory, and I thought I was home free.

Then I saw my oncologist, and the treatment options he laid before me seemed overwhelming. Again I was in the wilderness, not because God was leading me there, but because I ran there out of fear. God did not leave me alone. He gave me clear direction regarding the course of treatment to follow.

The big battle for me has been, and continues to be, in my

mind—not to let fear overwhelm me, not to dwell on the what-ifs, but to count on God's character and His promises, which are sure.

Lord God, You know my thoughts, my fears, and my frailties. You know how determined I am to follow You one minute and how fearful I am the next. I praise You for not giving up on me and for not leaving me in the wilderness. You keep meeting me where I am and providing for me there. Thank You for using the hard times in my life to show me Your steadfast love and faithfulness.

You are my sovereign Lord, who is in control of all things, large and small. You are my Good Shepherd, who knows the way, who calls me by name, and who knows my needs and provides for them even before I ask. How grateful I am for Your promise not to leave me desolate . . . You in Your grace and mercy come to me. Praise You!

Melinda Merwin
Homemaker

TODAY'S TIP: Recount the Lord's past faithfulness as you face present difficulties.

PRAYER REFERENCES: Psalm 139:2; Psalm 23; Luke 12:29–31; John 14:18

Let Go . . . Let God!

Trust in the Lord with all your heart and
lean not on your own understanding;
in all your ways acknowledge him,
and he will make your paths straight.

—Proverbs 3:5–6

On our wedding day, my husband and I gave each other a special gift. We each chose a Bible verse for our marriage and presented it during our vows. How wonderful that God directed Gordon to Proverbs 3:5–6, knowing cancer was in our future.

I love how the author of Proverbs said that we are to trust in the Lord and not lean on our own understanding, which is always flawed and based on human experience! How could I understand what God was doing when He called me to go through cancer? But in His infinite wisdom, He knew that cancer would produce fruit in my life. My own understanding of it was *human,* but His was *divine.*

When we acknowledge God as the giver of all good things and His wisdom as supreme over ours, He will set us on a straight path. It was nice to take my hands off the steering wheel and let God take over. How freeing that was to a woman who had to plan everything.

I praise You as my sovereign Lord. You, who created the heavens and the earth, created me and hold my life and breath in Your hands. You know the length of my days. I trust in You, my faithful and loving Lord.

How I thank You for Your goodness to me. You have done so many great things in my life. [Take a moment to thank Him for His specific provisions and gifts.] I am truly at rest when I consider all You have done.

I praise You as the Great Physician. You will designate the time and date of my healing. Every cell in my body is in Your hands. You graciously bestow Your goodness on those who take refuge in You. How great is Your goodness, which You have stored up for me because I trust in You.

Laura Geist

TODAY'S TIP: Give control of your life and your future to God. Let go . . . and let God!
PRAYER REFERENCES: Psalm 31:14–15; Psalm 116:7; Psalm 31:19

The "Big C" and the "Little c"

It is the name of Jesus which, through faith in him, has brought back the strength of this one whom you see here . . . that has restored this one to health.

—ACTS 3:16 NJB

Shortly after I was diagnosed with non-Hodgkin's lymphoma, I received an e-mail from my namesake niece, Susanne. She was a medical student at the time and is now a surgeon. Her message was simply, "Aunt Sue, I want the 'Big C' (Christ, that is) to conquer the 'little c' (cancer)." Instantly I responded with "Susanne, where did you find that? It's awesome." She replied, "I don't know. It just came to me." I wrote back, "Susanne, I will never refer to cancer as the Big C again."

My niece's words caused an instant change of perspective for me. Since then I have shared my "Big C" and "little c" stories with hundreds of others who have been equally touched. They seem eager to pass on the message or ponder it further themselves.

The "Big C" and the "Little c"

My niece's words serve as a lasting reminder of where the fullest healing power lies—in our Lord Jesus Christ.

Christ Jesus, my Lord, thank You for the gift of my life. Help me deepen in my desire to live with You as I cope with this cancer diagnosis and its many realities. I want to lean on You with all I am.

Lord, You invite me to ask for what I desire. I want to live well and learn all I can on this present path even though it's scary. It's hard to deal with so many unknowns and face times when I am not in control. But it's comforting to know that You want to walk with me one breath, one blink, one swallow, and one heartbeat at a time.

Help me focus on You as my "Big C," ready to crush and triumph over the "little c" that I am coping with now. Above all, I deeply desire that You are praised in this experience. If I can be assured of this, all that is happening is worthwhile for my growth and for Your glory.

Sister Sue Tracy
Hospital oncology chaplain

TODAY'S TIP: Look for a chance to share both your "Big C" and "little c" stories.

PRAYER REFERENCE: Acts 3:16

Hands Wide Open

*See, I have engraved you
on the palms of my hands.*
—ISAIAH 49:16

Late one evening, after my diagnosis, I couldn't sleep. I was thinking about all the what-ifs that could be coming down my path. I knew the "right" answer in my head: God was in control. Convincing my heart was another thing.

I had been reading Chuck Swindoll's book *Elijah*, and I came across a passage where Elijah had felt abandoned.[1] I was feeling much the same way that evening, fearful of the future, forsaken, and forgotten. I continued reading about Elijah that night, since we basically had something in common, then Isaiah 49:15–16 came to my attention. What a revelation to me that God had my name, Linda, written in the palm of his hand.

The diagnosis of breast cancer took me by surprise, but God was not surprised. He knew all along what was coming, but praise God, He was coming with me as we started the journey. This journey has taken me down some interesting paths, but one thing I know: the hand that holds mine has my name inscribed on it.

Lord, You oversee every detail of my life. You have assigned my portion and my cup. You have made my lot secure. In faith I can proclaim that You have caused my boundary lines to fall in pleasant places. Surely I have a delightful inheritance. I have set You always before me. Because You are at my right hand, I will not be shaken.

Father, although the journey I am on is not always easy, I thank You for holding me in Your arms when I am afraid and feel that the circumstances are overwhelming.

Help me to rest and trust You. I confess, Father, that I am not good at resting in You. Like an active two-year-old, I would rather be doing something than sitting still. Father, forgive me for my restlessness and prideful nature. Help me trust You to supply all my needs for each and every day. Thank You for Your help and presence!

Linda Pewitt
Homemaker

TODAY'S TIP: Surround yourself with a good support system. It is easier to give help than to receive it, but let your support team help you as you need it.

PRAYER REFERENCES: Psalm 16:5, 6, 8; Isaiah 49:16

God's Love Language

*One thing God has spoken, two things
have I heard: that you, O God, are strong,
and that you, O Lord, are loving.*

—PSALM 62:11–12

It was a rather bleak, Midwestern winter day several weeks after my cancer diagnosis and prior to my surgery. I decided to take a walk to get some fresh air, exercise, and time alone with God. That day, perhaps struck with the grayness all around me, I made a lighthearted request in view of all the heavy requesting I had been doing. I asked God for some flowers as a reminder of His love.

Shortly thereafter, God began to send me flowers . . . and flowers . . . and more flowers! At one point, we had so many floral arrangements in the living room that our daughters commented that it looked like a funeral home—yikes! As I opened the door to find yet another deliveryman or received fresh-cut flowers from a friend bringing dinner, I could hear God's tender "I love you" loud and clear.

These gifts of flowers continued right through my eight months of treatment. A friend celebrates each of my years as a cancer survivor with one more lavender rose. Such beautiful reminders of my Creator's love for me.

I praise You, Jesus, for showing Yourself strong and loving on my behalf. Thank You for the beauty of the world You have created for me to enjoy. The colors, textures, and aromas point me to You. The lilies of the field grow without laboring or spinning, yet not even Solomon in all his splendor was dressed like one of these. And I am grateful for Your wonderful lesson in this: that I am not to worry about tomorrow, for tomorrow will worry about itself.

Thank You that in the midst of all the cancer treatments, I can rest in Your love. Because Your love is better than life, my lips will glorify You. I will praise You as long as I live. I love You, Jesus, because You first loved me!

Elizabeth Jane
Homemaker

TODAY'S TIP: Watch for God's tender "I love you" in unexpected places.

PRAYER REFERENCES: Psalm 62:11–12; Matthew 6:28, 29, 34; Psalm 63:3–4

Peace or Panic

Jesus said, "Peace I leave with you;
My peace I give to you."
—JOHN 14:27 NASB

I was on my way to yet another doctor's appointment. Overwhelmed with all the information and appointments with doctors I had never seen before, I was being bombarded by giant fears—fears of being sick and alone.

All of a sudden a much-needed song began to play on my car radio. The words spoke right to my heart: "He knows how to care for what belongs to Him." I pulled over to the side of the road and started to cry. I said out loud to God, "I *do* belong to You. You are all I have. I know You are with me. But I'm so scared, and I need You."

No other messages came on the radio, but when I spoke *truth* to myself, my panic turned to peace. God heard me and answered me with His presence.

There were other times like that during my cancer experience. I had *panic* when I let all my fears come in and *peace* when my mind and heart looked to God and who He is.

Lord, thank You for Your promise to give strength to Your people.

You bless Your people with peace. I am amazed to consider that Jesus came to preach peace to those who were far away and peace to those who are near. For through Him I have access to You, a holy God.

When panic rolls over me like a giant wave, help me look to You. Help me turn from my panic and experience Your peace—a peace that transcends all understanding. Thank You that I can be assured that there is nothing to fear that comes from You. Help me rest contentedly in Your plan for me.

Right now, I claim [out loud], "I do belong to You. You are all I have. I know You are with me." Thank You for speaking Your peace to me.

Debbie Petersen
Women of Faith Conference Staff

TODAY'S TIP: Close your eyes and imagine Christ speaking "peace" to your heart.

PRAYER REFERENCES: John 14:27; Psalm 29:11; Romans 5:1; Ephesians 2:17–18; Philippians 4:7

All for His Glory

*They will see the glory of the LORD,
the splendor of our God.*

—ISAIAH 35:2

Enough! That was the feeling in our hearts when the doctor told us the diagnosis of my leukemia. During the three previous years, we had adopted two children, unexpectedly gotten pregnant, moved to Quebec for nine months of language study, and gone to the Ivory Coast, where we intended to work as long-term missionaries. Four weeks after arriving there, the country broke out into civil war and we were evacuated in a helicopter by U.S. and French Special Forces. With five children and very few belongings, we moved to a mission station in Togo to work for a year. Six months after our return to the States, I became ill. Initially we experienced a lot of "whys" and anger. *This*, after all we've just been through?

We were quickly reminded, however, of God's faithfulness to us through each of the huge and sometimes traumatic changes of the last few years. He would continue to hold us in the palm of His hand. We knew the answer to the "why?" and it was simple—so that we could once again experience

His amazing grace and plan, and so that He could be glorified through us.

Dear Father, thank You for Your faithfulness in the past. I know I can count on Your faithfulness in the present and future as well. I would not have chosen this path, but Your grace has been sufficient and will continue to be. Thank You for Your promise to strengthen my feeble hands and steady my knees that give way. I am so grateful that You say to my fearful heart, "Be strong, do not fear, Your God will come . . ." When I am weak, You are truly strong!

May Your power rest upon me, dwell in me, and flow out to others. Thank You for putting Your treasure in this jar of clay to show the all-surpassing power is from You and not me. Thank You for giving me the privilege of reflecting Your glory and being transformed into Your likeness with ever-increasing glory.

Kayleen Merry
Former missionary and teacher

TODAY'S TIP: Whatever your journey has been, picture yourself in the palm of His hand.

PRAYER REFERENCES: Isaiah 35:3–4; 2 Corinthians 4:7; 2 Corinthians 3:18

Firmly Held

*For I, the LORD your God, hold your right hand;
it is I who say to you, "Fear not, I will help you."*
—ISAIAH 41:13 RSV

When I was a little girl, my family would go to the beach. I remember my father taking me by the hand and walking with me toward the ocean. We'd wade out together. Sometimes the waves would break over my head and I'd be swept under, but never did my father lose his grip on me. He never let me go.

As I reflect on my cancer experience, I realize that my heavenly Father never let go of me either. He was with me as I waited for the diagnostic results and as I endured numerous treatments. He never left me, even though the waves of anxiety swept over me, blinding me to His presence.

The wait to be admitted into the stem-cell protocol seemed interminable, but God taught me that His timing is perfect. I ended up being in a different protocol than was originally planned, one that worked out for my good. It also resulted in my being in the hospital at the same time with someone from my Bible study. Not only did God provide for my medical care, but He provided a friend in the Lord, just down the hall!

Lord God, Your steadfast love never lets me go. When my hold on You is weak, Your grip on me is firm. Nothing can sweep me away from You, because You have made me Your child through Jesus Christ. You have swept away my transgressions like a cloud and my sins like mist. You have redeemed me and made me Your own forever.

Thank You for allowing me to call You my Father and for calling me Your child. Thank you that nothing can separate me from Your love—neither death nor life, neither angels nor demons, neither the present nor the future, nor any powers, neither height nor depth nor anything else in all creation will be able to separate me from Your love that is in Christ Jesus my Lord.

Melinda Merwin
Homemaker

TODAY'S TIP: Thank God for His firm grip on you, regardless of the size of the waves.

PRAYER REFERENCES: Isaiah 41:13; Isaiah 44:22; Romans 8:38–39

A 100 Percent Guarantee

Then you will know that I am the LORD;
those who hope in me will not be disappointed.
—ISAIAH 49:23

I remember when my oncologist told me I had about a 50–50 chance of surviving colon cancer. I desperately wanted some kind of guarantee that I would be OK. But that was impossible.

Plenty of people who offered me other "guarantees":

Eat certain natural foods, and they will cure you.
Drink a certain tea, and it will cure you.
Take certain vitamin supplements, and they will cure you.

But I am at heart a skeptical former newspaper reporter. I knew there was no way all these methods could deliver what they were promising. I wanted to believe that one of them really was the answer, but which one was it? What if I picked the wrong one?

And then I remembered: "Some trust in chariots [food and

drink] and some in horses [vitamins and herbs], but we trust in the name of the LORD our God" (Psalm 20:7).

It wasn't *which* had an ironclad guarantee; it was *Who*. My diagnosis, my treatment, my prognosis . . . and my future were in His hands. I had His guaranteed promise that when I put my hope in Him, I would not be disappointed.

Heavenly Father, forgive me for rushing about trying to find something that will give me complete assurance and guarantees. I know better than that. Instead, I want to seek You with all my heart and trust You completely. I acknowledge that You know every cell in my body and that You are in control. I praise You as my sovereign God and the Creator and Sustainer of my life.

Help me remember that no matter how many times I am cured of an illness, I still am going to die someday, and when that happens I really will be more alive than I have ever been!

I am so grateful that those who hope in You will not be disappointed. Help me make wise choices about what medical treatments to take and what possible complementary treatments to add. Let me choose things that will feed my body, mind, and spirit. Keep me from putting my trust and hope in anything but You. I humbly ask these things in the name of Jesus, the One who died for my sins and gave me life.

Lynn Eib
Author, *When God and Cancer Meet;*
Finding the Light in Cancer's Shadow

TODAY'S TIP: If you decide to investigate complementary treatments, don't take your focus off the only 100 percent guarantee, the Giver of Life!

PRAYER REFERENCE: Isaiah 49:23

God's Mercies
to Our Children

*If you then, though you are evil, know how to give good
gifts to your children, how much more will your Father
in heaven give the Holy Spirit to those who ask him!*
—LUKE 11:13

Luis and I decided to tell our four sons (then ages eleven to
seventeen) that I had cancer so that as a family and in a godly
way we could face whatever was ahead. There was a long
silence after we told them. Then Stephen cried, "But, Daddy,
people die from cancer!"

"That's true," Luis said, "but we believe God is going to
make Mom well. She won't be feeling as good as she did, so
it will mean some changes—for all of us. You guys will have
to learn to take care of yourselves and help your mother
every way you can."

Before my illness I cared fiercely for the whole tribe, looking
upon them as five helpless males who could not beat their way
out of a paper bag. That period of our lives made them much
more aware of the work involved in taking care of a home and

a family. They all benefited from having to take more responsibility because Mom couldn't do everything.[2] Now, twenty-five years later, I trust their wives are pleased with the results!

Father, You promise that all things work together for good for those who love You and are called according to Your purposes. You are using this trial to produce good fruit in my life and in the lives of many others, including my family.

Today, I want to pray for the children You have entrusted to me. Thank You for putting them in my life. Thank You for giving me the privilege of being their mother [or grandmother]. I trust You to work in their lives through this cancer journey. Use it to teach them, mold them, and shape them into godly young people and adults. I pray that You will guard their hearts and minds. Protect them from the evil one and from the fears the world will throw their way. Surround them with Your peace and Your love.

Use this time, Lord, to draw my children ever closer to You. Jesus said, "Let the little children come to me, and do not hinder them, for the kingdom of heaven belongs to such as these." I entrust them into Your care, as their only perfect Father!

Pat Palau
Cofounder, Luis Palau Evangelistic Association

⧉ TODAY'S TIP: Be comforted—God cares for your children even more than you do!

⧉ PRAYER REFERENCES: Romans 8:28; Matthew 19:14

A Warm Covering

He will cover you with his feathers,
and under his wings you will find refuge.
—Psalm 91:4

The radiologist called my husband into the room so we could talk. Though it was a hot August day, I felt cold lying on the examining table. As the conversation proceeded, my thoughts were racing. *Are we talking about the possibility of cancer? How can this be?* I lay there in silence and thought of my husband, who had already lost a dear wife to cancer, and of our three young children.

In that moment the voices in the room seemed muffled; no longer was I listening to the conversation. I sensed that I was being covered with a warm blanket. It started at my feet and slowly moved up to my shoulders. I strongly felt the warmth and heard a still, small voice saying to me, "Sue, I love you. I will never leave you or forsake you . . . you are Mine."

For many years I had known of the "peace of God which is far more wonderful than the human mind can understand" (Philippians 4:7 NLT), but on that August day I experienced that peace as a warm covering and a quiet reassuring voice, a peace that would carry me through my cancer journey.

You are my resting place. What a privilege it is to rest in the shadow of the Almighty. You are my refuge and my fortress, my God in whom I trust. You cover me with your feathers, and under Your wings I find refuge. Your faithfulness is my shield and rampart. I will not fear the terror of night, nor the arrow that flies by day . . . nor the plague that destroys at midday. For I desire to make You, the Most High, my dwelling. In Your refuge no harm will befall me. You know me and love me. You saw this day in my life, an ordinary day that would change me.

O God, You cover my head and protect me in the day of battle. Though I do not know what lies ahead, I know You and Your covering. I am comforted by Your hand of protection over me and around me. You are faithful; You will never leave me for even a moment. Thank You that I can rest in Your arms. I can trust You fully to take care of my family and me, one day at a time. I rest in Your peace, which will continue to guard my heart and my mind. In Jesus's precious name.

Sue Stalzer
Homemaker and teacher

☙ TODAY'S TIP: Have someone join you on your doctor's appointments. An extra pair of ears may pick up information you miss.

☙ PRAYER REFERENCES: Psalm 91:1, 2, 4, 9; Psalm 140:7; Hebrews 13:5; Philippians 4:7

No Fear of Bad News

Blessed is the man who fears the LORD . . .
He will have no fear of bad news;
his heart is steadfast, trusting in the LORD.
—PSALM 112:1, 7

Every time a doctor calls, my heart falls into my stomach. How I have struggled with fear! Because of this battle with fear, the Psalms have been my constant companion. One of my favorites is Psalm 112. In the Living Bible, verse 7 says, "He does not fear bad news, nor live in dread of what may happen. For he is settled in his mind that Jehovah will take care of him." The last part of the verse is the key, isn't it? It all boils down to my trust in my Creator. Do I really believe God will take care of me?

God's perfect love is hard to comprehend in a world where love has strings attached, is conditional, and is sometimes temporary. The Lord says, "I love you completely and forever." Jesus said, "If you then, though you are evil, know how to give good gifts to your children, how much more will your Father in heaven give the Holy Spirit to those who ask him!" (Luke 11:13).

My Lord is compassionate, kind, and full of love toward me. These truths are able to make my heart secure in His perfect plan when my fears threaten to sweep over me!

I praise You, Lord, for who You are. You are perfect in Your love. Your Word says that while I was still a sinner, Christ died for me. Your love is unconditional! You have proclaimed, "I will never leave you or forsake you." Your love is forever!

Thank You, Father, for lovingly taking care of me. I'm sorry for doubting You, for allowing my fears to sweep over me. I specifically agree with You about my following fears . . . [share your fears, big and small, with the Lord].

How grateful I am that I can cast these fears on You because You care for me. They are Yours, and You will deal with them in love. You, O Lord, have been faithful! I praise You that I can put my trust in You! How I praise You that Your perfect love casts out my fears!

Susan Sorensen

TODAY'S TIP: Pinpoint your greatest fear. Ask God to help you find a promise in the Bible that addresses it.

PRAYER REFERENCES: Romans 5:8; Hebrews 13:5; 1 Peter 5:7; 1 John 4:18

Seeing God in the Rainbows of Life

Whenever the rainbow appears in the clouds,
I will see it and remember the everlasting
covenant between God and all living
creatures of every kind on the earth.

—GENESIS 9:16

It was all so complicated. My previous medical conditions of weakening connective tissues and brittle bones didn't help matters. As a forty-three-year-old single woman, I was feeling overwhelmed and alone as so many factors had to be considered to determine my best treatment for breast cancer.

I kept praying for God's direction and peace. I went for a second opinion at another medical facility, and this second doctor prescribed the exact situation as the first. I was grateful for this confirmation and that my mom and my sister had gone with me for moral support.

The three of us had gone through a rainstorm to get to that appointment. As we began to head home, we were amazed that over the horizon we could see two rainbows completely arched one on top of the other. The colors were vivid, and the overall effect was breathtaking. It seemed to follow us all the way home. My mom said it was a sign from God that everything was going to work out for good—a promise from God of His love and faithfulness.

You are King of heaven and earth. Thanks to Your Holy Word, I can picture You sitting on Your throne—with "the appearance of jasper and carnelian. A rainbow, resembling an emerald, encircles the throne. Surrounding the throne are twenty-four other thrones, and seated on them are twenty-four elders. They are dressed in white and have crowns of gold on their heads. From the throne come flashes of lightning, rumblings and peals of thunder." You and Your throne room are full of glory—and a rainbow!

Thank You for the reminders and signs of Your love in this life. You have me in the palm of Your hand and guide me through the maze of details that I don't understand. Thank You for the hope I can have that even in the storms of life, You are able to make rainbows!

Susan Wilkinson
Kindergarten teacher

TODAY'S TIP: Sometimes a setback is really a setup for a comeback. After the storm comes a rainbow, a promise of God's love and faithfulness.

PRAYER REFERENCE: Revelation 4:3–5

Death of a Dream

For as the heavens are higher than the earth,
so are My ways higher than your ways,
and My thoughts than your thoughts.
—Isaiah 55:9 NKJV

As I lay on an exam table and was told the result of my upcoming treatments, tears streamed down my face. The intense chemotherapy and total body radiation I needed to destroy the cancer would also destroy my ovaries. It was hard to swallow that I would not be able to have any more biological children. I thought, *This is so unfair! I am only twenty-four years old.* My dreams of having four biological children were slipping away. We had our newborn daughter, Julie, whom we were so thankful for, but it wasn't in our plans to have only one child.

Six years later we pursued adoption, and our sweet Josiah was given to us in only five weeks' time. He was definitely more than we ever could have dreamed for. He has brought so much joy to our family. Even though my dream of having three more biological children was taken from me, God had an even better dream for our family.

Lord, Your thoughts and ways are far above mine. You know the plans You have for me, plans to prosper me and not to harm me, plans to give me hope and a future. Your dreams are definitely better than any I could have planned. It is a great comfort to my soul that You always want the best for me.

I praise You that nothing is impossible for You. I may look at a situation with my human eyes, but You have an infinite way—a plan that has no boundaries, no human limitations. I lay my dreams before Your throne . . . [Take time to name them if you can.] Help me let go of those dreams You desire for me to let go of. Give me a glimpse of the better paths You have planned for me. How grateful I am that I can trust You with my life and dreams!

Trina Mavin

Pastor's wife and homemaker

TODAY'S TIP: If your cancer trial causes the death of a dream, it is OK to cry and grieve. But don't stop there! Ask God to give you new dreams.

PRAYER REFERENCES: Isaiah 55:9; Jeremiah 29:11; Psalm 113:9

Suffering: God's Megaphone

*The God of all grace, who called you to his
eternal glory in Christ, after you have suffered
a little while, will himself restore you and
make you strong, firm and steadfast.*

—1 PETER 5:10

As for most, the diagnosis of cancer hit me like a ton of bricks. However, I don't recall going through the so-called stages of grief. If I did, I progressed through them in rapid succession, to arrive and linger at *Why me?* Then, instead of *Why me?* it became *Why not me?* After all, God had blessed me and spared me from so much. How could I question His will for my life, when at thirty-three, I was diagnosed with ovarian cancer?

C. S. Lewis once said, "God whispers to us in our pleasures, speaks in our conscience, but shouts in our pains; it is His megaphone to rouse a deaf world."[3] I was hearing God's voice loud and clear. He used my momentary suffering not only to conform me more to Christ but to put my focus on eternity.

God gently reminded me of all Christ had suffered—the perfect example of how I should endure trials. And He assured me of what awaited me on the other side of suffering when one day I will be permanently restored!

You are holy and righteous, the Almighty Refiner, and with You, there are no mistakes. Even though this journey may be difficult, I am grateful and expectant that You will use it to help me be more like You.

Lord Jesus, thank You for all You suffered on my behalf. You knew the suffering that was to come when You went to the cross, the agony of being separated from Your Father, and still you chose, willingly and obediently, to see it through.

I am so grateful that I can rest in the fact that nothing will happen to me that hasn't first passed through Your hand. I praise You, Lord, that You are the anchor that holds me secure, no matter what suffering may come. You are my Rock and the eternity in which I can be absolutely assured.

Sherri Schut
Sales representative

TODAY'S TIP: Thank God in faith for how He is going to use this cancer journey in your life and in the lives of others.

PRAYER REFERENCES: Hebrews 6:19; 12:2; 1 Peter 5:10

Silent

O my God, I cry out by day, but You do not answer, by night,
and am not silent. Yet You are enthroned as the Holy One.

—PSALM 22:2–3

God was silent. I had prayed and prayed and received no comfort. The mastectomy was over, and I was numb with fear. Fear ruled my heart. After reading all the books I could find on breast cancer, I was still fearful of the future. I was convinced I was going to die and not see my four grandchildren mature to adulthood. I cried and begged God to give me courage. He was silent.

After my third chemotherapy session, I attended a wonderful weekend retreat at my church. I took the opportunity to discuss my fear of dying with the leader. She looked me straight in the eye and asked, "When did God tell you that you would die of cancer?" I told her that God had been silent. She responded in the tone of an amused parent, "Do you understand now?"

It suddenly became clear! I had been consumed with things I did not know and would not know unless God chose to reveal them to me. I realized that God wanted *me* to be silent and to entrust my future and its unknowns into His faithful care.

Lord, You look from heaven and You see me. You have fashioned my heart. Your eye is on those who revere You, on those who hope in Your mercy. I do hope in Your mercy to deliver my soul from death and to keep me alive in these difficult and dry times. My soul waits for You. My heart rejoices in You because I trust in Your holy name.

I praise You, Lord, that I can unload my fears and worries at the foot of Your throne. I get weighed down by all the unknowns. [List specific ones you are struggling with; place them before Him.]

Thank you for taking care of all that concerns me. Help me trust You completely and not get ahead of You. I praise You for carrying me through this season of unknowns and for teaching me how to trust in the midst of Your silence.

Jan Parker
Retired judge

TODAY'S TIP: Trust God when He speaks and when He is silent.

PRAYER REFERENCE: Psalm 33:13–22

He Is Able to Make My Way Perfect

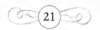

It is God who arms me with strength and makes my way perfect.

—PSALM 18:32

I waited, not knowing if I would need chemotherapy or not. One oncologist told me I was in a gray area but recommended it to be safe. Then a second opinion at another hospital said I did not need chemo. You may be thinking, *That must have been a huge relief.* Not really! How was I to know which way to go? What if I didn't do chemo and regretted the decision later? What if I did it for no reason? These questions swirled around in my head. I was clinging to Psalm 18:32—that God would make my way perfect—but I couldn't imagine how He would do it.

On the exact day that a decision had to be made, a small bit of information was revealed that caused one oncologist to reverse his decision. He decided I did not need chemo. I never expected that to happen.

As I look back, the Lord was gracious and faithful. He provided in a way that I did not need to second-guess my decision. He brought me to a place where everyone agreed. He made the way perfectly clear.

Lord, You are a perfect God. Who is God beside You? And who is the Rock except my God? I praise You as a shield and refuge. How grateful I am that I can find a safe haven in You. I can rest in Your love for me.

I thank You, in faith, that You will make my way perfect, that You desire to do that for me. I confess I often try to make my own way or even think my way is more perfect. Forgive me for . . . [List any specific areas.] I praise You for Your cleansing and forgiveness through Jesus Christ.

Father, You are my sovereign Lord. I know that all things come through Your hands. You allow things in my life for a greater purpose than I often understand. I thank You for Your promise that You will work all things together for good. You are in the process of molding and making me more Christlike. As I go through this process, I know You will get me to where I need to be. Thank You for making my way perfect.

Susan Sorensen

TODAY'S TIP: Are you facing a big decision? Ask God to make your way perfect. He will!

PRAYER REFERENCES: Psalm 18:31–32; Romans 8:28

Is Your Face Turned Toward Me?

The LORD bless you and keep you;
the LORD make his face shine upon you
and be gracious to you; the LORD turn
his face toward you and give you peace.

—NUMBERS 6:24–26

The night before my surgery, I lay in the stillness and remembered a pastor's story I'd heard. He told about a little boy who awoke, frightened in the night. The boy toddled off to find his parents and woke up his father with his mournful sobs.

The father returned to the son's bedroom with him and promised to lie down beside the little boy's bed until the child fell asleep again. They lay there in the darkness awhile, and then the little boy whispered, "Daddy? I can't see you. Are you still there?"

"Yes, Son, I'm here."

The boy lay still a moment, and then the father heard his voice again. "I can't see you, Daddy. Is your face turned toward me?"

"Yes, Son, my face is turned toward you."

That's what I wanted to know throughout that long night in the hospital. *Are You still there, God? Can You see me? Is Your face turned toward me?*

And the answer was the same one I heard all my life: *Always!*[4]

Lord, You promise to bless me and keep me. You make Your face shine upon me and are gracious to me. How comforting it is to know You actually turn Your face toward me and give me peace. Your eyes are on those who trust in You, on those whose hope is in Your unfailing love. Your eyes are on me!

Even in the stillness and darkness of night, when no one is with me, You are there. Thank You for the promise that those who look to You are radiant; their faces are never covered with shame.

Barbara Johnson

Best-selling author, *Plant a Geranium in Your Cranium*

TODAY'S TIP: Whisper the little prayer, "Whatever, Lord." These two words have lifted me out of life's cesspool many times.

PRAYER REFERENCES: Numbers 6:24–26; Psalm 33:18; Psalm 34:5

Safety in the Lion's Den

God rescues and saves people and does mighty
miracles in heaven and on earth. He is the one
who saved Daniel from the power of the lions.
—Daniel 6:27 NCV

When my husband and I were told that the recommended treatment began with six sessions of chemotherapy, I felt my body begin to disconnect from my mind. Then I thought of the prophet Daniel. He had been told by King Darius that he was to face a den of lions, although he had obeyed God. I shouted in my head, *My doctor is throwing me into the lion's den, and I've done nothing wrong!*

Throughout the weekend before that first chemo treatment, I wrestled with thoughts of escaping—seeking refuge. Certainly, Daniel must have thought the same thing! Gradually, I began to hand everything over to the Lord, and I asked Him to be my rescuer. Later, when the last treatment was administered, I realized that God *had* protected me from the drugs that were designed to destroy the good and the bad within my body.

Darius's words to Daniel resonated in my heart: "May the

God you serve all the time save you!" (Daniel 6:16 NCV). I emerged practically unscathed by the many possible side effects. God *was* victorious over the "lions" that were meant to ravage my body!

I praise You and thank You, dear Lord, for rescuing me from that which might harm or destroy me. When my mind and body become weak, You graciously lift me up and give me strength. You bring me up out of the horrible pit, out of the miry clay. You set my feet upon a rock and establish my steps. You put a new song in my mouth—a hymn of praise to You, my God.

I thank You for the doctors and nurses who have been called to care for those suffering from illness and disease. But I marvel at Your power and might, that You can overcome the worst of these infirmities.

Lord, may I remember this season of my life and recall Your loving and merciful touch. May I always reach for You when I need rescuing from life's trials and tribulations. Thank You for allowing me to discover this wonderful thing about You: You are the living God, and You endure forever.

Katherine Powers
Sales administrative assistant

TODAY'S TIP: When you feel the lions' breath on the back of your neck, look to the One who enabled Daniel to emerge from the den without a scratch.

PRAYER REFERENCES: Daniel 6:16; Psalm 40:2–3

He Will Quiet You
with His Love

The LORD your God is with you, he is mighty to save.
He will take great delight in you, he will quiet you
with his love, he will rejoice over you with singing.
—ZEPHANIAH 3:17

The fitted mask was carefully placed over my head and snapped into place. It was so tight it left crisscross marks on my face after it was removed. Once again it was time for another treatment on an inoperable brain tumor. Gratefully, a year of chemo was over, and now I was on a new journey of radiation treatments for six weeks.

It was critical that I lie very still on the table. How would I use the next twenty minutes? I knew it was important to put myself in the Lord's hands. When I closed my eyes, I learned to shut out the clutter from my thoughts and focus on my Lord. He held me secure, and I felt protected and peaceful in the center of His love. I was caught up in His love as we shared fellowship in prayer, Scripture, and songs of surrender and praise.

As each radiation treatment came, there was no foreboding but an anticipation of a special time with the Lord.

Lord, I come in prayer, thanking You for Your presence. I place myself in Your care. As I focus on You, my heart is full of love and praise that You give me mercy and grace just when I need it.

Thank You for Your comfort during the times of solitude and for the sweet fellowship we have while those treatments are doing their work. You endured the cross and cleansed me from sin and gave me a new life in Christ. I praise You as One mighty to save. How grateful I am that You are quick to quiet me with Your love. You even rejoice over me with singing!

Thank You for the open door to share and minister to patients, nurses, technicians, and doctors. Lead me, Lord. I want my life to point to You and bring glory to Your name.

Joyce Wright
Coauthor, *I'll Love You Forever*

TODAY'S TIP: During your day, focus on the Lord and walk close with Him.

PRAYER REFERENCE: Zephaniah 3:17

Fearfully and Wonderfully Made

For you created my inmost being; you knit me together in my mother's womb. I praise you because I am fearfully and wonderfully made.

—PSALM 139:13–14

My mother-in-law introduced me to the art of quilt making. My first experience with sewing was a vain attempt to make a skirt in seventh grade. I believe it was actually supposed to fit someone! That early failure convinced me I would never learn to sew. But twenty years later, the process of choosing fabrics and sewing them into beautiful patterns became an exciting, creative pleasure. I enjoy every aspect of putting together a quilt. It may seem crazy that one would spend so much time cutting material into little pieces only to sew them back together again!

How comforting to know that God is the Master Creator. He has a unique plan for me. He has taken all the bits and pieces of my life—including some that are not so pretty, like cancer. He knows how they all fit together and how the quilt of my life will look in its final design. He makes each quilt unique, special and of the highest quality. I am so grateful that the very One who made me is in control of my life!

Thank You, Lord, for making me just the way You did. You created my inmost being. You knit me together in my mother's womb. I praise You because I am fearfully and wonderfully made. My frame was not hidden from You when I was made in the secret place. When I was woven together in the depths of the earth, Your eyes saw my unformed body. All the days ordained for me were written in Your book before one of them came to be. How I praise You for Your intimate knowledge of me and Your perfect plan!

Although I cannot comprehend the intricacies of Your creative hand, I know I can lay my burdens at Your feet and entrust my future into Your care. You know my afflictions and fears. All I have to do is call on You, and You hear me, love me, and uphold me. You have promised to watch over me now and forever. I rest in You, Lord, and trust in Your power and promises. Thank You for enfolding me with Your warm blanket of love.

Mary Beth Buhr
Piano teacher and homemaker

TODAY'S TIP: As you slip under your quilt tonight, realize that God is enfolding you with His warm blanket of love.
PRAYER REFERENCE: Psalm 139:13–16

Are You Sure, Lord?

*Lead me in the right path, O LORD, or my
enemies will conquer me. Tell me clearly what
to do and show me which way to turn.*
—PSALM 5:8 NLT

The night before my double mastectomy and reconstruction,
my children gave me two silver bracelets specially designed and
engraved with Psalm 5:8 and Psalm 50:23. This surgery was the
culmination of many prayers, research, and wise counsel. The
bracelets were a reminder of how God leads us very specifically and how He had led me.

There was a time when, instead of the direction becoming
clearer, I was becoming confused. I needed wisdom. I also
needed God to calm my racing heart. After arriving home
from one of my consultations, I immediately went out on the
deck to pray. I told God I needed to hear from him. Then I
began reading in my Bible where I had left off the day before.
The next chapter was Psalm 5, and when I came to verse 8, I
knew He had heard my cry for help.

I was overwhelmed to the point of tears as I was once
again assured He would lead me, tell me, and show me! My

heart rejoiced, and later that day I knew for certain the path before me.

Lord, I thank You for the confidence I have when I turn to You for guidance. You are faithful! I know You desire that I be right in the center of Your will even more than I do. You will tell me what to do and show me which way to turn. I am greatly comforted by the fact that You care personally about me and that I don't have to be anxious about the decisions I make.

I am grateful for Your love letter to me: the Bible. You give me direction through it. Your words are a lamp to my feet and a light for my path. Help me trust You for what is ahead that I cannot see. You know all and care for me perfectly. Continue to direct my footsteps according to Your will and Your promises. Thank You for the comfort Your words bring to my soul!

Sarah Eggerichs
Vice president, Love & Respect Ministries, Inc.

⊰ TODAY'S TIP: Look for God to guide you in some way this day. Thank Him ahead of time!

⊰ PRAYER REFERENCES: Psalm 119:105, 133; Psalm 94:18–19

Climbing into
God's Chariot

*He who dwells in the shelter of the Most High
will rest in the shadow of the Almighty.*
—PSALM 91:1

Hannah Whitall Smith, in her classic book *A Christian's Secret to a Happy Life*, said trials are "God's chariots sent to take the soul to its high places of triumph." She encouraged, "When your trial comes, then, put it right into the will of God, and climb into that will as a child climbs into its mother's arms. The baby carried in the chariot of its mother's arms rides triumphantly through the hardest places, and does not even know they are hard. And how much more we who are carried in the chariot of the 'arms of God!'"⁵

I was reminded of this on the morning of my mastectomy. The entire way to the operating room a tall, strong orderly sang many of the great Christian hymns as he navigated my gurney through the hallways. I might have believed him to be an angel, but everyone seemed to know him as he walked by! His voice and message were beautiful.

I truly felt I was in God's chariot all the way to surgery. I had climbed in, and my loving Father was reminding me of all His great promises as we rode on our way.

I praise You, heavenly Father. Though sin separated me from You, You grabbed hold of me and made me Your child. I praise You, Jesus, for taking my place on the cross and being the bridge to this wonderful, eternal relationship. How awesome it is to be loved so completely.

Thank You for allowing me to climb into Your arms. I can let go and let You hold me through this ride down a path that is unknown. Help me to trust You so completely that I don't even know the rocky places are hard.

Praise You for Your promise to work all things, even the bad things, for good for those who love You and are called according to your purpose. All I need to do is give my needs, desires, and wants to You, my faithful and loving Father, the God in whom I trust!

Susan Sorensen

TODAY'S TIP: Watch for the unexpected blessings— gifts the Lord desires to give you during this journey!

PRAYER REFERENCES: Romans 5:8; Romans 8:28

Crucified with Christ

*I am crucified with Christ and I no longer live,
but Christ lives in me. The life I live in
the body, I live by faith in the Son of God,
who loved me and gave himself for me.*
—Galatians 2:20

Tears filled my eyes when a nurse came to check on me. She thought I was upset about surgery, but I was not. They were tears of gratitude for the orderly who wheeled me all the way to surgery singing my favorite hymns. She was pleased to hear about my "chariot" ride!

She then shared with me something very interesting. During a mastectomy, the patient's arms are spread horizontally like Jesus's were on the cross of Calvary. She felt it was a unique identification with Christ. Later, I was hit by Paul's words in Galatians 2:20, "I am crucified with Christ." In essence, I am laying my desires, my thoughts about what is best, and my dreams at the cross. My life is no longer about me, but about my faithful, sovereign God.

How easy it is for my selfish desires to creep in and get in the way of my complete surrender to God. This is a new beginning of being crucified with my Lord. He doesn't want a selfish child. He wants Christ living in me to the praise of His glory.

Thank You, Lord, that when I became a Christian I became a new creation. You discarded the former way of life and put a new, clean heart in me. You began Your work and will carry it on to completion until the day of Christ Jesus. Thank You for the transformation You have begun in me. I confess that my selfish ways and desires have often gotten in the way of Your desire for me. Forgive me for . . . [Take a moment to confess any areas where you have not submitted to God's plan for you.]

How grateful I am for Your promise to cleanse me if I simply confess my sin to you. Thank You for this opportunity to be crucified with Christ. It is no longer I who live, but Christ who lives in me. I worship You as my loving Father who walks with me on this road to maturity in Christ. I worship You as the Sustainer and Provider who is more concerned about my growth than my cushy life! I praise You, my faithful and powerful Lord.

Susan Sorensen

TODAY'S TIP: Reflect on all that it means to be "crucified with Christ."

PRAYER REFERENCES: 2 Corinthians 5:17; Philippians 1:6; Galatians 2:20; 1 John 1:9

Be Still

Be still, and know that I am God.
—Psalm 46:10

"Be still." These were the words I heard again and again throughout my radiation therapy. After the technicians positioned me on the table, they'd say, "Be still. Don't move." Then they would leave me alone in the radiation therapy room for ten to fifteen minutes at a time. Little did they know that these frequent instructions to be still just served to remind me of the instructions God had given me in Psalm 46:10 on the very morning of my first treatment.

"And know that I am God." The second part of that verse kept ringing in my mind every time they repeated their directions to me. He is God! He is the Lord Almighty, the blessed controller of all things (even the beams of radiation I feared would damage my heart and lungs), my ever-present help (even when left alone in the room of radiation equipment), my strong tower, my fortress, the Maker of heaven and earth.

He continued to lovingly remind me with every "be still" that He wanted me to relax in His strong arms and trust in His personal care for me.

Almighty God, You orchestrate the details of my life to remind me that You are indeed in control and will never leave me or forsake me. Where can I go from Your Spirit? Where can I flee from Your presence? You discern my going out and my lying down. You are familiar with all my ways . . . Your right hand will hold me fast. Thank You for putting me in the place where all I can do is be still and depend on You. I want to soak up Your joy and strength.

Loving Father, I confess that my thoughts tend to race to all the things to be anxious about rather than trusting You. Yet You are the Lord of the entire universe. You tend Your flock like a shepherd. You gather the lambs in Your arms and carry them close to Your heart. You gently lead those who have young. Thank You for being such a tender shepherd!

Lynne Davis
Homemaker

TODAY'S TIP: The next time you find yourself having to be still, turn your thoughts toward your tender Shepherd, who is always with you.

PRAYER REFERENCES: Psalm 139:3, 7, 10; Isaiah 40:11

Hair Today, Gone Tomorrow

But if a woman has long hair, it is a glory to her.
—1 Corinthians 11:15 NKJV

When I was seven years old, I got my fantasy doll for Christmas. With a twist of a button, I could make Velvet's hair shorter or longer. I always wanted to grow long, luscious locks, but my mom insisted a pixie cut was right for me. Though short, my hair was thick, shiny, and beautiful—a treasured family trait.

Then cancer came along. "It's not too bad; the worst part is losing your hair," my oncologist said. My hair? Hair loss meant I was losing the centerpiece of my appearance!

I was encouraged to cut my hair very short to ease the loss. Three days before Christmas, I was taking a shower and noticed a small clump of hair on the drain cover. As I looked down, the word *peace* popped into my head. The next day, I found a larger clump of hair. *Peace of God!* cried the voice in my head. Each day, I experienced the "peace of God, which surpasses all understanding" (Philippians 4:7 NKJV).

God was in charge of the thing I dreaded most. He knew peace was what I needed to get through this tumultuous loss without Velvet's button to make my hair grow back.

God, You are the Prince of peace. You quiet the raging seas of my fears with the perfect peace of Your Holy Spirit. I praise You as the One who sits over all circumstances, even what feels like a flood. You are enthroned as King forever. You give strength to Your people and bless Your people with peace. Thank You for Your faithfulness in the storms of life and for the gift of unexplainable peace in the midst of them.

Lord, I lay my appearance before Your throne. I stand amazed that You know how many hairs are on my head and how many I will lose as I battle with cancer. I thank You for teaching me the meaning of true beauty through this. You desire the inner beauty of a gentle and quiet spirit, which is of great worth in Your sight. Thank You for Your love and patience toward me as You peel away layers of vanity and pride. I praise You for the gift of Your peace that passes all understanding!

Laura Geist

TODAY'S TIP: Tie a bandanna or scarf around your head before putting on a hat. It will make your hair loss less noticeable

PRAYER REFERENCES: Psalm 29:10–11; Matthew 10:30; Philippians 4:7

Unmistakable

*Now as they observed the confidence of Peter and
John, and understood that they were uneducated
and untrained men, they were amazed, and began
to recognize them as having been with Jesus.*
—ACTS 4:13 NASB

Having cancer was like being in love: it was all I could
think about. Every brain cell was consumed with thoughts of
the disease, and every fiber of my body bore witness to its
presence. My oldest child had stood in the doorway to my
bedroom and sniffed. Wrinkling her nose, she exclaimed, "It
smells like the hospital in here. You smell like chemo!" The
chemical odor was undeniable, making its way through the
pores in my skin. I quietly seethed with resentment at this
total takeover of my life. As the treatment dragged on, cancer
seemed to have become my identity.

Then, in my pondering, I began to think about what it
would be like if, instead of cancer, Jesus became my identity.
What would it be like if my brain cells were consumed with
His thoughts and if my life gave off a sweet fragrance, unmis-
takably His? What would my life look like if He made a total

takeover? What impact would it make on my world if I were recognized as having been with Jesus?

Father God, I didn't sign up for this. Some days are pretty OK, but some are really tough. Yet I will consider this whole cancer deal worth it, if in the end I look more like Jesus, sound more like Him, even smell more like Him. I want it to be obvious that I've spent time with Him. It's worth it, if somehow I can honor You by going through this experience, whatever the outcome. So I'm asking You to make it worth it. Make me more like Jesus. Make it undeniably evident that You are at work in my life. Honor Yourself.

Help me to see this illness from Your perspective. There's a lot I don't understand, so I'm trusting You. I can't see down the road, so I'm grateful You know the beginning from the end and everything in between. Even on days when I think I'm holding on to You, I realize it's Your grip on me that's keeping me together. Thanks for Your unmistakable grace.

Thanks to You, Lord God, who always leads me in triumphant procession in Christ and through me spreads everywhere the fragrance of the knowledge of Him!

Joanne Arentson
Wife, mom of three teenagers,
women's ministry director

TODAY'S TIP: Enjoy some new perfume and be reminded that God is at work in your life, creating a sweet fragrance.

PRAYER REFERENCES: Acts 4:13; 2 Corinthians 2:14

Cancer Isn't Very Funny

*A cheerful heart is good medicine, but a
broken spirit saps a person's strength.*
—Proverbs 17:22 NLT

When I was first diagnosed with cancer, I honestly wondered if I would ever laugh again. It was hard to imagine having a really good belly laugh over anything. That's why when I came home from the hospital, I sent my husband to the video store to get me every Pink Panther movie he could find. You may not enjoy Peter Seller's slapstick comedy as the bumbling Inspector Clouseau, but I always have found it impossible to watch and not laugh. So I watched them all. I laughed through them all. And it was *very* good medicine.

I am not one who believes laughter always can cure what ails you, but I definitely believe a cheerful heart is good medicine. My Bible footnotes say the literal translation of Proverbs 17:22 is "a cheerful heart causes good healing."

It is a real understatement to say that cancer isn't very funny. But it's not an overstatement to say that we can find joy and even laughter in the midst of cancer. You have to look for it, and sometimes you have to even create it for yourself . . . so go ahead and send someone to the video store!

Lord, I pray that You will give me a cheerful heart, in spite of all I've gone through and all that still is ahead for me. I know I don't have to smile and pretend I'm happy and that everything is all right. But I do want to feel Your quiet joy in me and even hear laughter from my lips. I want to remember that there is life after and even with cancer.

Please help me not be dejected and sad, for the joy of the Lord is my strength. And Holy Spirit, please develop in me the fruit of joy— a joy that's not based on my circumstances, but on my relationship with my Father. Let me be joyful in the simple gift of another day to love and be loved.

I pray, Lord, that You will bless me and protect me, that You will smile on me and be gracious to me, that You will show me Your favor and give me Your peace.

Lynn Eib
Author, *When God and Cancer Meet;*
Finding the Light in Cancer's Shadow

TODAY'S TIP: It's *impossible* to tickle yourself, so get some help to tickle your funny bone—watch a comedy or hang out with a funny friend. Laughter, like yawning, is contagious!

PRAYER REFERENCES: Proverbs 17:22; Nehemiah 8:10; Numbers 6:24–26

My Chemo Buddy

*Therefore, as we have opportunity, let us do good to all,
especially to those who are of the household of faith.*
—GALATIANS 6:10 NKJV

Trina called me right away when she heard of my cancer.
"Laura, do you have anyone to take you to chemo?" I was taken
aback. Who would want to sit there for two hours watching
someone hooked up to a chemo IV? But for Trina it was a new
ministry.

Trina would pick me up half an hour before my treatment
every three weeks for six months. We had a little routine. I'd sit
in one of the large recliners. She'd get me juice and cookies.
We'd chat and catch up on what was happening with our children and solve all of the world's problems. She would adjust my
favorite pillow so I'd be comfortable. Then she'd bring maga-
zines for herself so I could sleep at the end of my treatment.
We'd usually sneak in lunch before the chemo hit my system.

I had mixed emotions about chemo. I hated what it did to
my body, but I looked forward to the special times with Trina.
Her Christlike attitude and positive outlook made such a dif-
ference during those valley experiences of treatment.

Praise to You, my God and Savior, who daily bears my burdens. How thankful I am that You know my every need and care for each one. I praise You that You give power and strength to Your people.

You have blessed me by putting me in the pathway of people who care for me. Thank You for sending committed friends here on earth who walk with me during this difficult journey and are a tangible expression of Your presence.

I wait in hope for You, Lord, because You are my help and shield. In You my heart rejoices, for I trust in Your holy name. May Your unfailing love rest upon me even as I put my hope in You.

Laura Geist

TODAY'S TIP: Ask a friend to join you on for your chemo appointments. If you are a survivor, consider being a "chemo buddy" to someone undergoing treatment.

PRAYER REFERENCES: Psalm 68:19, 35; Hebrews 13:5; Psalm 33:20–22

The Reservoir

If we don't know how or what to pray,
it doesn't matter. He does our praying
in and for us, making prayer out of
our wordless sighs, our aching groans.
—ROMANS 8:26 MSG

For years, I had made a habit of Bible reading and prayer. It was second nature, it seemed. But now, in the face of incessant, chemo-induced nausea and fatigue, my Bible sat collecting dust on the bedside table and my thoughts were consumed with simply trying to breathe without throwing up.

I felt like an abject failure in my relationship with God, convincing myself that if I tried just a little bit harder or pushed myself a little bit more, surely I could navigate this treatment with greater success. If I was just a little tougher, I could read and recall what I read and pray for those whose circumstances were more difficult than mine. Surely, I could.

Somewhere in the midst of my self-accusation and do-better cajoling, grace entered in, and I began to remember that God did not change when I was diagnosed with cancer, nor did He suddenly become dependent on or impressed by my performance. His Spirit was still busy doing what He said He'd do: continually interceding on my behalf.

Father, how grateful I am that my life with You does not depend on my performance. Thank you for pouring out Your mercy and grace on me and for giving me peace that is beyond understanding. I am in awe of You when I consider that in my weakness and inability, Your Spirit is my knight in shining armor, my hero, coming to my rescue, talking to You on my behalf. Thank You for letting me lean hard on You during these tough times. In fact, thank You for these tough times that teach me to trust You.

You are my reservoir of strength and power. When my river runs dry, You wait patiently to fill me up with Yourself. Glory to You, Father!

Joanne Arentson
Wife, mom of three teenagers,
women's ministry director

TODAY'S TIP: When it's hard to pray, allow music to draw your soul into God's presence.

PRAYER REFERENCE: Romans 8:26

As the Shepherd Gathers His Lambs

He tends his flock like a shepherd:
he gathers the lambs in his arms
and carries them close to his heart.

—Isaiah 40:11

When my children go through difficult situations, I find myself drawn closer to them. My instinct is to surround them with love and pray more intensely for them. That is exactly what God has done for me and my family during my cancer journey.

Two weeks after my bilateral mastectomy, our family moved from North Carolina to Michigan. I began my aggressive chemo treatments with a whole new set of doctors. Those days and circumstances were, from the beginning, more than I could bear. I often felt (and still do!) like a little girl cuddled up in my Father's arms with my head buried in His great chest and my ear pressed hard enough to hear His heart beating. I have experienced His love in ways that I've never known before.

I have been blessed by words of Mary Prentiss Smith in her poem "Lean Hard":

> Child of My love, lean hard,
> And let Me feel the pressure of thy care;
> I know the burden, child, I shaped it:
> Poised it in My own hand, made no proportion
> In its weight to thine unaided strength;
> For even as I laid it on, I said
> I shall be near, and while he leans on Me,
> This burden shall be Mine, not his.[6]

Father, thank You for the privilege of crawling into your arms and laying my head on Your chest. You desire to encircle me with Your love, comfort me, and be my strength. How priceless is Your unfailing love! Both high and low among men find refuge in the shadow of Your wings. Like them, I am able to feast on Your abundance. You bless me from Your river of delights. For with You is the fountain of life, and in Your light I see light.

Lord, I confess that I allow these anxieties to storm over me. I feel myself crawling down from Your lap to chase after these troubles, taking my life into my own hands. Please gather me back into Your arms and help me to allow You to carry me through these difficult times.

You are my Shepherd, I shall not want. You make me lie down in green pastures; You lead me beside quiet waters. How grateful I am that You restore my soul!

Julie Kuntzman
Wife and mother

TODAY'S TIP: Remember, the Father is never closer to the vine than when He is pruning it.

PRAYER REFERENCES: Isaiah 40:11; Psalm 36:7–9; Psalm 23:1–3

Beauty Shop Blues

*Your beauty . . . should be that of your inner self,
the unfading beauty of a gentle and quiet spirit,
which is of great worth in God's sight.*

—1 PETER 3:3–4

A week after I was diagnosed with cancer and facing the prognosis of losing my hair, my husband and I had the opportunity to hear Randy Travis sing his hit song "Forever and Ever, Amen." We looked at each other in awe when we heard the words: "They say time takes its toll on a body; makes a young girl's brown hair turn gray. But honey, I don't care; I ain't in love with your hair, and if it all fell out, well, I'd love you anyway."[7]

While I still had hair, I decided to join my girls in getting hair wraps while vacationing in Florida. When I began to notice my hair falling out following my first chemo treatment, I'll admit I felt a bit emotional, but we laughed ourselves silly when I quickly turned my head and my hair wrap went flying across the room!

When we realized the loss of all my hair was inevitable, our two young girls set up a beauty parlor, complete with cash register, soft music, and two pairs of safety scissors. They had a good time until they stood back and looked at their creation. It was definitely not one of my better haircuts!

Thank You, Jesus, for the gift of laughter. I am grateful for the opportunities to laugh even in the midst of difficult circumstances. Thank You for those who laugh with me and keep laughing when I need it most.

Help me always keep my eyes on You, and not on the temporal things of this world. May my inner beauty be the unfading beauty of a gentle and quiet spirit. May it reflect You, bringing glory to You.

I praise You for the sheer joy of coming before You. I come to You with thanksgiving and praise You with music and song. For You are the great God, the great King above all gods. I bow down in worship and kneel before You because You are the One who made me.

Elizabeth Jane
Homemaker

TODAY'S TIP: Get a great wig, and enjoy never having a bad hair day!

PRAYER REFERENCES: 1 Peter 3:3–4; Psalm 95:1–3, 6–7

When There's Nothing
You Can Do

*Praise the LORD, I tell myself; with my
whole heart, I will praise his holy name.*
—PSALM 103:1 NLT

My first round of chemo literally almost knocked me out.
Not only were the cancer cells under attack, but I also developed numerous infections, including pneumonia. I was on
oxygen and had barely enough strength to move. Fevers raged.

One night as I tossed in bed, sweaty and in pain, it struck
me that there was *nothing* I could do. I couldn't take care of
the children. I couldn't help my husband with the load he was
carrying. I couldn't even carry on much of a conversation. I
was useless!

Then the words hit me: *Praise the Lord*. Even with a body
that seemed wasted and a heart that ached, I could bless the
Lord. I could offer my silent praise to Him—and offer Him
my body, mind, and emotions. This was all I could do, but I
had an overwhelming sense that He was pleased.

Lord, I am so thankful that You simply desire my praise. You are pleased with a sacrifice of praise when there is nothing else I can do. So here I am to bless You.

Praise the Lord, O my soul; all my inmost being, praise Your holy name. Praise You, O my soul, and forget not all Your benefits . . . who forgives all my sin and heals all my diseases, who redeems my life from the pit and crowns me with love and compassion, who satisfies my desires with good things so that my youth is renewed like the eagle's.

You are compassionate and gracious, slow to anger, abounding in love. You do not treat me as my sins deserve or repay me according to my iniquities. For as high as the heavens are above the earth, so great is Your love for those who fear You; as far as the east is from the west, so far have You removed my transgressions from me. As a father has compassion on his children, so You have compassion on me . . . from everlasting to everlasting Your love is with those who fear You. Praise You!

Kayleen Merry
Former missionary and teacher

TODAY'S TIP: Meditate on Psalm 103 and practice praise.
PRAYER REFERENCES: Psalm 103:1–5, 8–13

The Gift of Suffering

*For it has been granted to you on behalf of Christ
not only to believe on him, but also to suffer for him.*
—PHILIPPIANS 1:29

One of the greatest gifts I received through my cancer journey was something I had never asked for and didn't really want. It was the gift of being able to identify with the sufferings of Christ.

In my religious upbringing, this was not something I contemplated or desired. In fact, I probably would have thought of suffering as punishment for sin and something to be avoided. But I began to see God's redemptive plan being carried out in my life through suffering. I grew in my understanding of what Madame Guyon said: "I have learnt to love the darkness of sorrow; there you see the brightness of His face."[8]

My first chemotherapy treatment was scheduled for Good Friday. Before it began, I asked Jesus to allow me to reflect on His suffering as I remembered His death. Moments later, the nurse came to access my newly implanted port for the chemo drugs. As she did so, the pain was very intense. With my eyes closed and tears running down my face, I could very clearly see Jesus and the pain that He felt as the nails pierced His hands and feet.

Thank You, Jesus, for the incredible physical suffering that You were willing to undergo for me. Thank You that though You are God, You did not consider equality with God something to be clung to, but rather made Yourself nothing, taking on the very nature of a servant as a human being. Thank You for humbling Yourself and becoming obedient to death—even death on a cross.

You tell me that as Your child and heir, I will share in Your sufferings in order that I may also share in Your glory. Help me consider my present sufferings as not worth comparing with the glory that will be revealed.

Thank You for giving me the privilege of coming to You . . . that in my suffering I can fix my eyes on You. For the joy set before You, You endured the cross, scorning its shame, and sat down at the right hand of the throne of God.

I ask for the grace to grow in my understanding of what it means to identify with Your sufferings.

Elizabeth Jane
Homemaker

TODAY'S TIP: Find the joy Jesus offers as you "embrace your cross."

PRAYER REFERENCES: Philippians 2:6–8; Philippians 1:29; Romans 8:17–18; Hebrews 12:2

Carabiner of Hope

39

*We also rejoice in our sufferings, because we
know that suffering produces perseverance;
perseverance, character; and character, hope.*
—ROMANS 5:3–4

When I was recovering from my cancer, I bought a carabiner. "What's that?" you may be asking. "Some new medical device?" Actually, a carabiner is used in mountain climbing to connect ropes. It's the number one choice to assure that ropes are held securely. It protects the climber by making the lifelines safe.

Life has been full of challenges that seemed like mountains. I have learned a lot along the path. There have been times I have relied on the easiest choice because it seemed like a fast fix for a tough climb. Then I hoped it was safe. Other times I have tried to do it on my own, without securing my rope. I've experienced numerous challenges in life without a firm hold.

My carabiner reminds me of the only secure and steadfast lifeline: Jesus. When I attach myself to Him, He will never let me go. He is the vision beyond my sight. I may have times of feeling helpless, but I am never hopeless when I am securely hooked to and held tightly by Him.

Dear Lord, I confess, I am not always brave. I forget to hold on to You when the journey is rough and my climb is uphill. [Take a moment to acknowledge before the Lord those times when you have gone your own way or tried to do it without His aid.] Thank You for holding on to me—for protecting and loving me even when I have not secured my rope to You. I am grateful for Your willingness to receive me now.

You are my safe and steadfast lifeline. You hold me secure. You do not grow tired or weary, and Your understanding no one can fathom. You give strength to the weary and increase the power of the weak. Even youth grow tired and weary and young men stumble and fall. But those who hope in You will renew their strength. They will soar on wings like eagles. They will run and not grow weary. They will walk and not faint.

Laurann Patterson
Homemaker and retired teacher

TODAY'S TIP: Find a symbol that reminds you of where your hope should be.

PRAYER REFERENCE: Isaiah 40:28–31

My Sanctuary

40

*Consider the ravens: They do not sow or reap, they have
no storeroom or barn; yet God feeds them. And how
much more valuable you are than birds! Who of you by
worrying can add a single hour to his life? Since you cannot
do this very little thing, why do you worry about the rest?*

—LUKE 12:24–26

When we bought a new house, my only request was a screened-in porch. Little did I know how important that porch would become to me three years later, when I was diagnosed with late-stage ovarian cancer. The porch became my recovery room as well as my sanctuary where I could sit, worship, reflect, and meditate on God's wonderful creation.

One of those creations was the birds. They flew so gracefully, sang so melodiously, and ate from my feeders so thankfully. I knew God was watching over them, yet I was much more valuable than they in His sight! What a comfort and peace that brought me on days when I was bald, weak, and weary from fighting this disease. There were days I did not feel like reading or singing, but I could enjoy the birds singing God's promises to me.

Seven years later, I'm still enjoying my screened-in porch. I look forward to entering my peaceful sanctuary and enjoying God's presence and creation.

Heavenly Father, thank You so much for creating this wonderful world for me to live in. Thank You for sending the birds to sing, the trees that grow tall and point to the heavens, the beautiful blue skies, and even the gray and rainy days. These are gifts from You. All I have to do is receive and enjoy them.

Open my eyes, Lord, in days when I am too weak to care. Help me see Your wondrous works in all the nature around me. Help me also release my worries to You because You ask me, "Who of you by worrying can add a single hour to his life?" I know from the Bible that all of my days were numbered even before I was born. It is up to me to make the most of every day You give.

Thank You for the "sanctuaries" where I am able to enjoy the gifts that are given by You, my Creator.

Diane Lankford
Insurance agent

TODAY'S TIP: Do something that makes you smile today, even if it is sitting under a tree or listening to the birds sing.

PRAYER REFERENCES: Luke 12:25; Psalm 139:16

A Win-Win Situation

*For to me, to live is Christ
and to die is gain.*
—PHILIPPIANS 1:21

Someone sent me a newspaper article about a pastor who was diagnosed with a rare and aggressive form of cancer. The pastor admitted that when the doctors told him that cancer had invaded his body, his knees buckled.

Yes, I thought when I read that line, knowing exactly how that pastor felt. *Our knees buckle. And that puts us in exactly the right position to ask God for help and to feel His hand resting on our lives.* It's at times like these we need to remember this advice: don't forget in the dark what you've learned in the light.

It is not that any of us would *choose* to have cancer. But as Christians, we're in a win-win situation. Some wise wordsmith put it this way: "The worst that can happen is the best that can happen."

Surely the worst that can happen is that we die—and that's actually the best that can happen, because we know we don't go from life to death. As singer Kathy Troccoli says so emphatically, when we die, we go from life to *life*.[9]

A Win-Win Situation

Lord, I praise You that when I sigh out my last earthly breath, I will breathe in the glorious atmosphere of heaven. Thank You for the promise of eternity with You. For You will come down from heaven, with a loud command, with the voice of the archangel and with the trumpet call of God and the dead in Christ will rise first. After that, we who are still alive will be caught up together with them in the clouds to meet You in the air. And so we will live with You forever. What an amazing day to look forward to!

How grateful I am that You walk with me on the path of life—a path that will eventually bring me to glory. I pray I will be like Enoch of the Old Testament, who walked with You and was no more because You took him away. I know that as I keep walking with You, one day we will be closer to Your house than to mine—and that will be a glorious beginning!

Barbara Johnson
Best-selling author,
Plant a Geranium in Your Cranium

TODAY'S TIP: Heaven is not just pie in the sky by and by. It's steak on the plate while you wait![10]

PRAYER REFERENCES: 1 Thessalonians 4:16–17; Genesis 5:24

The Unwrapped Gift

*All the members do not have the same function,
so we, being many, are one body in Christ,
and individually members of one another.*
—ROMANS 12:4–5 NKJV

God equips each one of us with special gifts and talents to be used for His glory. It was neat to see how God directed people to use their gifts to minister to me when I needed it most. I saw this with my sisters. Jennifer filled my freezer with meals. Janice organized my kitchen better. Margie kept in touch with phone calls and accompanied me to difficult appointments.

Friends also provided practical help. Molly did our family's laundry during my treatment weeks. At first, I cringed at the thought of this precious woman having to touch our dirty socks! But turning her down was denying her a chance to use a talent of homemaking that God had given her. Another friend, Tammy, decorated my home for Christmas.

I truly believe that God sent people with special talents to care for me. By accepting their service, I was giving them a chance to obey God and exercise the gifts He had given them.

It also allowed them to participate in the healing that God was doing in my life.

Gracious God, You give gifts to Your people so that we are prepared for works of service. You desire that the body of Christ be built up in unity and in service to one another through the use of our gifts.

Lord, thank You for equipping each of your children with different gifts and talents. I thank You for the people who willingly offer those talents to me. Help me to humble myself and accept the offer to use their gifts in my life. I pray that You will be glorified as these precious saints give of themselves.

You are able to make all grace abound to me, so that in all things at all times, having all that I need, I will abound in every good work. You faithfully provide. Praise You!

Laura Geist

TODAY'S TIP: You cannot do it all. Don't deny others the opportunity to minister to you with the gifts God has given them.

PRAYER REFERENCES: Ephesians 4:12–13; 2 Corinthians 9:8

Bolder as I've Gotten Balder

*Therefore, since we have such
a hope, we are very bold.*
—2 Corinthians 3:12

Who ever would have thought that boldness would come with baldness? Certainly not me! Being a woman who likes to look good, I thought being part of the Bald and the Breastless would keep my head under the covers. I thought I would be afraid to come out and go about the days God ordained just for me. What a picture of His sweet grace in my life! With marriage, motherhood, and ministry, it has been hard to squeeze cancer into my schedule. I've been able to push those covers back and get out of bed looking the way I do!

To my surprise, God used cancer not to slow me down but to accelerate my desire for others to know Him. While life is difficult for those of us who know our good God through a personal relationship with Jesus Christ, what are other women doing who don't know Him? What are they modeling behind closed doors to their precious children watching? We cannot give out what don't have! We have everything to offer a hurting world when we love Christ. We can boldly live the hope within us.

Lord Jesus, how comforting to know that You are so personal, You know the number of hairs on my head and not on my head. Only You can give me the ability to face these days with such big physical strikes against my femininity. You graciously give me boldness and courage that only You can give. I don't have it on my own. You are the reason I get out of bed every morning looking and feeling the way I do. How grateful I am that I have everything to offer those you place in my life because I have You. I can be bold and courageous because You are the hope within me.

I praise You, Lord, with all my heart. I praise Your name for Your love and Your faithfulness. You have exalted above all things Your name and Your Word. When I called, You answered me. You made me bold with strength in my soul. Though I walk in the midst of trouble, You revive me; You stretch out Your hand to help me. You perfect that which concerns me. I am so grateful to be Yours!

Kim Newlen

Author, speaker, and

founder of Sweet Monday

TODAY'S TIP: Find whatever headdress that makes you feel your boldest self, and go out and live the hope within you.

PRAYER REFERENCE: Psalm 138:1–3, 7–8

The Children's Prayers

We do not lose heart. Though outwardly
we are wasting away, yet inwardly we are
being renewed day by day. For our light and
momentary troubles are achieving for us an
eternal glory that far outweighs them all.

—2 CORINTHIANS 4:16–17

*D*ear God, please don't let Grandma Diane need chemotherapy."
"Dear God, please don't let Grandma Diane go bald."
"Does Grandpa know you have no hair under that hat?"

We mature ones are sometimes like them, aren't we? Our prayers are like children's—we want the bright side for our life, and we struggle to see God's light on these difficult subjects. In our medical treatments we are learning, growing, and knowing in a way as never before. We can scarcely fathom the verse above: that these troubles are "light and momentary" compared with the glory of eternity.

How very reassuring to my heart were the words of little Brooke, who ran to me from the airline bus and said in my ear: "Grandma, you look all right!"

Do I really grasp the truth of His holy assurance? Do I

need the positive human input so badly? Is this all bigger than I can see?

The Message translates the above passage: "On the outside it often looks like things are falling apart on us . . . on the inside, where God is making new life, not a day goes by without his unfolding grace. These hard times are small potatoes compared to the coming good times, the lavish celebration prepared for us"!

Yes, my loving Father, I need to grow up. My prayers need to grow up. I am like a child in my desires, and I usually don't see the bigger picture. Help me to see Your greater perspective and to pray with confidence because of Your total loving care. Let me hold Your Word before my eyes and heart to focus on the eternal glorious events ahead.

I praise You for the hope of eternity. Praise to Your name that I can awake in the night and sing in my heart and mind: "Praise the name of Jesus . . . He's my rock, He's my fortress, He's my deliverer. In Him will I trust." Thank you for Your Spirit, who lives in me and lifts my soul above fear to a place where I experience Your unfolding grace.

I love You, My Savior, Lord, and King!

Diane Willis
Campus Crusade for Christ staff, counselor

TODAY'S TIP: Put today's verse on the bathroom mirror, near the kitchen sink, or in your purse.

PRAYER REFERENCE: 2 Corinthians 4:16–17

The Eternal Now

Teach us to number our days aright,
that we may gain a heart of wisdom.
—PSALM 90:12

Slow me down, Lord. I'm going too fast." That was my heart's cry. But life had been so full of the "busies"—all there was to *do* for the Lord—rather than simply *being still* in His presence. Was cancer part of the learning God had for me? Is that what it took to slow me down? Those days of quiet, rest, and radiation enabled me to get in touch with that part of myself that I longed for . . . the "Mary" who chose to sit at the feet of Jesus, basking in His presence, instead of the "Martha" who must always be *doing*.

What an opportunity to reassess my days, to be reminded that they are just what they need to be for God's purposes in my life. His plan for me has been unfolding since the beginning; for with God, each moment is an eternal *now*. Therefore, I have all the time needed to be about His business in a way that will bring Him glory. But that will only happen as I am still before Him, making each moment a moment for eternity.

Lord, this is the day You have made for me to rejoice and be glad in! I praise You for Your control over everything. Thank You for Your patience when I am acting like Martha, upset about many things. You gently remind me that only one thing is needed. Mary chose it: to sit at Your feet. You promise that this is better than anything and cannot be taken away from me. Truly, one day in Your courts is better than thousands elsewhere.

You are my light and my salvation—whom shall I fear? You are the stronghold of my life—of whom shall I be afraid? For in the day of trouble You promise to keep me safe in Your dwelling; You hide me in the shelter of Your tabernacle and set me high upon a rock. Thank You for slowing me down so that I am able to experience Your glorious presence!

Marti Odle
Area director for Community Bible Study

TODAY'S TIP: Reflect on ways you might spend your days more wisely.

PRAYER REFERENCES: Psalm 118:24; Colossians 1:17; Psalm 84:10; Luke 10:41–42; Psalm 27:1, 5

Angel Wings

*The angel of the LORD encamps around
those who fear him, and he delivers them.*

—PSALM 34:7

The nurse came in at four in the morning to hang my next bag of chemo. She was just a little overly awake when she began her cheerleading chant, "Go, chemo, go!" *Doesn't she realize what time it is?* I wondered. She then talked about visualizing the chemo as PacMan, gobbling up the cancer cells. That just didn't do it for me—computer games have never been my cup of tea, and least of all PacMan. The nurse left as happily as she had come in, and I was left to try to get back to sleep.

The next day I started thinking about what was significant to me—something I could visualize to help tolerate the chemo. My thoughts landed on angels. I envisioned angels with wings curled around their bodies to form a circle, and then I imagined them racing down my blood vessels sifting out the bad cells. A little later I found a resin angel that exactly fit my description. I bought it and placed it by my hospital bed to remind me that the angel of the Lord encamps around me and delivers me.

Lord, You have been kind and gracious to me. I praise You for the many good things You have done according to Your compassion. You became my Savior. In Your love and mercy, You redeemed me and carried me.

Lord, thank You for Your angels that minister peace and strength to me. When I cry and feel an absolute loneliness, I know You weep with me and that You sit right by my side. Fill me with Your power and presence to overcome the cancer cells in my body. Race through me to conquer and rescue! May I not leave You for one moment, for Your holy presence wraps me in angel wings.

Let me hear the rustle of angel wings that keep me from falling into self-pity and doubt. Thank You for Your promise to put angels in charge of me to watch over me wherever I go!

Kayleen Merry
Former missionary and teacher

TODAY'S TIP: Visualize something that reminds you of the Lord's protection and presence.

PRAYER REFERENCES: Isaiah 63:7, 9; Psalm 91:11

Sleep Deprived

*I will both lay me down in peace, and sleep:
for thou, LORD, only makest me dwell in safety.*
—PSALM 4:8 KJV

I had always been a morning person and followed the old adage, "Early to bed, early to rise." But cancer treatment changed that.

At first I thought it was worry or fear that was keeping me awake long hours in the night. However, after committing every single thing I could think of to the Lord, I was still awake. I asked people to pray for me. I was still awake. Finally, checking with my doctor (Now isn't that a novel idea?), I found out that sleeplessness is a common side effect of cancer treatment.

Patients undergoing radiation and many of the chemotherapy protocols find they cannot sleep. You want to go to sleep. You want to rest. You are bone tired. But your brain will not shut down. In talking with other cancer survivors, the most common comment was, "I thought it was just me."

I found that National Geographic travel videos or Moody Bible Institute praise and worship videos helped me through sleepless nights. My Bible was a source of encouragement.

Praying also brought comfort and courage during those long, sleepless nights.[11]

Lord God, I praise You that when I am awake in the middle of the night, You are not asleep. Even in the night hours, You hear my prayers. Your presence comforts me. Your Word strengthens me. I thank You, Lord.

It is amazing to consider that You watch over me. You are the shade at my right hand. The sun will not harm me by day or the moon by night. You watch over my coming and going both now and forevermore. Thank You for Your promise that when I lie down, I need not be afraid; when I lie down, my sleep will be sweet. You are my strength and my shield. You are my Shepherd. I will trust in You.

Lois Olmstead

Author, *Breast Cancer and Me*

TODAY'S TIP: Read 2 Chronicles 20 and copy verses of comfort on index cards to read during troubling times.

PRAYER REFERENCES: Psalm 121:3–8; Proverbs 3:24

Do You Trust Me?

*For great is your love, higher than the
heavens; your faithfulness reaches to the skies.*

—PSALM 108:4

My husband had moved ahead of us to start his new job in
another state. Our children were in bed and I was lying awake,
unable to relax enough to fall to sleep. I remember crying out
to God to calm my anxious spirit.

In those next minutes, I didn't hear God's audible voice, but
I know it was Him speaking to my heart: *Julie, if Dave called
you to say that he couldn't give any specifics except that he had a special date planned, would you trust him that the date would be good?*

I thought about that question. *If I don't trust him, then I'm
questioning Dave's love for me. I know that Dave loves me . . . so, I
guess my answer is yes, I would trust him.*

Then God's second question came: *Will you trust Me for the
outcome of the pathology report on the lumpectomy?*

My heart raced as I thought about that question! *Lord, if I
don't trust You, then I'm doubting Your love for me. I do know that
You love me . . . so, yes, I will trust You.*

I cannot adequately describe the calming peace that God

poured into my whole being at that very moment! Within a few minutes, I fell asleep.

How grateful I am that I can relinquish my anxious heart into Your trustworthy and loving arms. You are the God of hope, and nothing can touch me before it passes through Your hands. Lord, You make me stand firm in Christ. You have placed Your seal of ownership on me. You have put Your Spirit in my heart as a deposit, guaranteeing what is to come.

Fill me with joy and peace as I trust You so I may overflow with hope by the power of the Holy Spirit. Thank You for the light You shed on the journey as I need it and for the brightest hope in the midst of the darkest of days. I praise You that Your love is higher than the heavens and Your faithfulness reaches to the skies. Thank You for Your loving care of me.

Julie Kuntzman
Wife and mother

〰 TODAY'S TIP: Do you trust God's love for you? He is trustworthy!

〰 PRAYER REFERENCES: 2 Corinthians 1:21–22; Romans 15:13; Psalm 112:4, 7, 8; Psalm 108:4

Grace in Time of Need

*"My grace is sufficient for you, for my power
is made perfect in weakness." Therefore I will
boast all the more gladly about my weaknesses,
so that Christ's power may rest on me.*

—2 Corinthians 12:9

Throughout my entire breast cancer ordeal, I kept asking the Lord, "How am I going to get through this?" The assurance that came into my mind again and again was, *My grace is sufficient.* I did not doubt that the grace of Christ had made me His for eternity, but I wanted control over the situation and to know the outcome from the beginning.

My faith was tested by the absolute dependency I felt throughout my battle with cancer—a dependency on medical professionals, on loved ones to help me, and on the Lord. I am a woman who plans, organizes, second-guesses outcomes, and manages situations. None of those skills served me during the struggle. Only the sufficient grace of the Lord upheld me.

Now that several years have passed, sometimes, like Paul, I boast of the weakness I experienced, of weakness gradually growing into strength as the Lord defeated the monster —was it cancer or doubt? Both can kill the joy and hope in our lives. Christ wants us to have life abundantly in all circumstances. His grace is sufficient.

Heavenly Father, teach me to accept the grace You have provided —the grace that sees me through every day, every trial, every danger. Your Spirit upholds me when I am most fearful and weak. Thank You for Your promise to be faithful in my time of need. I am grateful Your treasure is in this weak vessel, made strong by the all-surpassing power that is from You and not from me. Teach me the joy of the hidden life You sustain in me and the victory You provide.

You are the only unchanging and solid place where I can run. You arm me with strength and make my way perfect. You train my hands for battle. You give me Your shield of victory, and Your hand sustains me. You broaden the path beneath me, so that my ankles do not turn. I praise You for Your overflowing and sufficient grace! Thank You, Lord.

Sandra Burmeister
University executive director

TODAY'S TIP: Imagine how your body feels filled to the brim with God's grace.

PRAYER REFERENCES: 2 Corinthians 12:9; 2 Corinthians 4:7; Psalm 18:31–36

Giving Thanks Is
Quite a Sacrifice!

Giving thanks is a sacrifice that truly honors me.
—PSALM 50:23 NLT

When my son severely broke his leg while playing baseball in the eighth grade, his heart broke over the loss of a dream. With major surgery and months of rehab on his horizon, I realized I could not fix his leg or his dream. Then *my* heart was breaking! I knew it was God's will that I give thanks in all things, but this didn't feel like something for which to be thankful. That's when I learned about a sacrifice of praise. When Abraham was asked to sacrifice his only son on the altar, he was asked to give God something very precious. Therefore, it was called a sacrifice.

Ten years passed between my son's disappointment and my cancer diagnosis. I had praised God when I didn't feel like it more times than I could count. Each time I offered a sacrifice of praise, I knew I was honoring God, even though my circumstances did not always change. Something was happening in the heavens and something was happening in my soul. Author

Carole Mayhall once told of the time she gave thanks when she didn't feel like it. She then reflected on how nine days later, her emotions caught up with her obedience!

Lord, I thank You that whether I feel like giving thanks or not, You are pleased when I offer a sacrifice of thanksgiving. Through Jesus I have the privilege of continually offering to You a sacrifice of praise. This isn't about feelings but about obedience. Just as Abraham offered a sacrifice without knowing the outcome, I, too, want to trust You even though I can't see the final score. It is so reassuring to know that even though I may not feel thankful, I am bringing honor to You and Your name, and that is my highest goal in life. So today I want to begin or continue the practice of giving thanks because I want to truly honor You. Thank You that I can trust You to help me do this.

Thank You for how You change my heart when I act in obedience. I praise You for the privilege of entering Your gates with thanksgiving and Your courts with praise. I give thanks to You and praise Your name. For You, O Lord, are good, and Your love endures forever. Your faithfulness continues through all generations.

Sarah Eggerichs
Vice president, Love & Respect Ministries, Inc.

TODAY'S TIP: Every time you don't *feel* thankful, give thanks!

PRAYER REFERENCES: Psalm 50:23; Hebrews 13:15; Genesis 22:1–19; Psalm 100:4–5

In Sickness and in Health

Submit to one another out of reverence for Christ.
—Ephesians 5:21

The experience of surgery and chemotherapy was so intense that I found it easy to be extremely self-absorbed. Yet we were a family. I had a husband and four sons to remember. The way I communicated reality, God's deliverance from pure terror, the capacity to live in the now, and the absolute confidence in God's character—those things all mattered to me, but they also mattered to my husband and children. I couldn't retreat but had to embrace life with my family.

At some point, I was struck by the realization of how difficult this was for my husband. He shared in a sermon once how he wept quietly and cried out to God for strength on the day we looked at cancer up close and personal. I realize now that he could have used a little more of the kind of support and comfort I received. He was always strong, confident, positive, and quick to move into areas of family life that had always been mine. But I'm sure he felt pulled in opposite directions. I often prayed that the Lord would sustain him as He graciously sustained me.

Almighty God, thank You for the gift of my husband. Sometimes I am so consumed with my needs that I am not adequately meeting his. I know he hurts when I hurt. Comfort him, Lord. Help him and strengthen him. Multiply his time and give him a heart of wisdom.

You have a clear directive for my husband: to love me as he loves himself. I can't imagine how this is possible right now, but I do know You are the God of the impossible! This is not a natural kind of love but a supernatural kind of love, a love that only You can create and manifest. Fill my husband with it so that he is able to love me like You ask.

And Father, You have told me to respect and reverence my husband —to notice him, regard him, honor him, prefer him, venerate and esteem him, praise him, and admire him exceedingly. This is a tall order! Fill me up with your enabling power to do this with joy even while I am going through cancer treatments. Help me fix my eyes on Your power to do exceedingly abundantly beyond what I ask or think.

Pat Palau
Cofounder, Luis Palau Evangelistic Association

TODAY'S TIP: Do something special for your husband or simply say, "Thank you."
PRAYER REFERENCES: Ephesians 5:22–32; Luke 1:37; Ephesians 5:33 (Amplified Bible); Ephesians 3:20

Joy in the Journey

*Be strong and courageous. Do not
be terrified; do not be discouraged,
for the LORD your God will be
with you wherever you go.*

—JOSHUA 1:9

After I had settled into a chemo chair, I commented to the woman in the chair next to mine that we needed an invention to help chemo patients keep their wigs on straight.

"Pantyhose," she said confidently.

Sure she had misunderstood me, I said, "I meant to keep our *wigs* from slipping," I said loudly.

"The thing that works best for me is pantyhose," she said again, smiling brightly.

I just smiled and nodded, assuming her brain tumor was a little more advanced than mine. She saw the look and explained, "You cut the legs off then wear the crotch on your head like a cap," she said. "It stays put, and you can pin your wig to the pantyhose."

"Oh!" I said, laughing at the image. Then I had an idea. "We could make a business out of it," I mused. (Later a friend even suggested a name for our enterprise: Chemo Crotches!) There in the chemo room, we erupted into gales of laughter.

Driving home later, I had to smile, remembering how I had laughed with the lady next to me. Then I recalled my friend Debbie's fax that morning: *I'm seeing Jesus sitting beside your chemo chair . . .* [12]

Thank You, Lord, for giving me back my bubble of joy in the unlikeliest places. That's just like You, Jesus, to turn my fear into cheer. Thank You for this gift that I can't seem to muster up . . . for anointing me with the oil of joy. Please use me to be an encouragement to other women going through this, even the woman I may sit beside during my next treatment. Help me give some other fearful person the gift of laughter in this journey through cancer treatment.

How grateful I am that I can face calamity and crisis with hope. I can face cancer with courage. In Your presence I find Your wonderful grace for the next breath—and for the next day and the next. And even better, You will use my affliction for something good. You will bring me through it—in spiritual healing if the physical healing doesn't come. Either way, You promise that my faith will be stronger, and I will know I am redeemed forever.

Barbara Johnson
Best-selling author, *Plant a Geranium in Your Cranium*

TODAY'S TIP: In this life, pain is inevitable, but misery is optional! Purposefully *choose* to be joyful. [13]

PRAYER REFERENCE: Psalm 45:7

Thirst Quencher

As a deer pants for the water brooks,
so pants my soul for You, O God.
My soul thirsts for God, for the living God.
—Psalm 42:1–2 NKJV

As I went through my eight rounds of chemotherapy, I remember being constantly thirsty. I always kept a big container of water within arm's reach. As the chemicals were zapping the cells within me, my body needed to be replenished by the cool, clean water.

I think that's the kind of picture God paints of Himself in the Bible. We are to thirst after the refreshment God can bring. I love how the psalmist emphasizes that it is not just a god, but the *living* God that we thirst for. In John 4:13–14, Jesus tells a Samaritan woman at a local well that He can provide her with *living* water. He says, "Whoever drinks of this [well] water will thirst again, but whoever drinks of the water that I shall give him will never thirst" (NKJV).

Jesus is the living water from the living God. He is the refreshment our tired souls need at the end of self-centered futility. Just as drinking water is essential to bodily functions, we can't function spiritually without Jesus's love washing over us.

O God, I earnestly seek You. My soul thirsts for You. My body longs for You in a dry and weary land where there is no water. I have seen You in Your sanctuary and beheld Your power and Your glory. Because Your love is better than life, my lips will praise You as long as I live.

How grateful I am that You are a cold, refreshing drink of living water on the parched path of my life. What an amazing promise that I will never be thirsty again when I drink of Your goodness and mercy. You are the fountain of water springing up into everlasting life. I know as I come before You, You will wash me with Your love and soothe the wounds that I carry. O Lord, give me a drink of Your water!

Laura Geist

TODAY'S TIP: Fill a large pitcher of ice water in the morning and drink it by a certain time each day. You can add a squeeze of lemon or lime to give it more flavor.

PRAYER REFERENCES: Psalm 42:1–2; Psalm 63:1–2; John 4:13–14

A Lamp unto My Feet

Your word is a lamp to my feet
and a light for my path.

—PSALM 119:105

S top!" I yelled. No one had told me what to expect during a full body scan. I'm slightly claustrophobic and was unprepared to be strapped to a table with a machine one-sixteenth of an inch above my face. I could think of only one way to get through the next hour and a half. I quickly asked permission for my husband to read to me from the Bible. I closed my eyes and listened to God's Word as the machine hummed quietly. I was completely at peace and unaware of the procedure—and even more amazing, unconcerned with the outcome.

I would later find out that in spite of surgery, I still had cancer. The ensuing radiation treatment required complete isolation in a hospital room for several days. The things I brought in would be thrown away at the end because they would be radioactive. I didn't want to bring my Bible. Instead, I entered isolation with twelve significant passages photocopied in large font. I spent my time reading those pages again and again. God's Word goes with us wherever we go and brings comfort in the midst of even the most uncomfortable moments.

Father, the Bible is so important to me. I thank You that through it, You give me wisdom and an understanding of my salvation through faith in Jesus Christ. All Your words are God-breathed (inspired by You!) and useful for teaching, convicting, correcting, and training me in righteousness, so that my thoughts become Your thoughts and my actions, Your actions. You have provided Your love letter to humankind so that I may be fully equipped for every good work. I praise You for revealing Yourself to me, for teaching me, correcting me, blessing me, and carrying me through.

I praise You for giving truth through Your words. How grateful I am that through them You graciously sustain and comfort me. How gracious You are when I cry for help. When You hear me, You answer me. Though I walk through difficult times, You promise to light my way. You will teach and lead me. Whether I turn to the right or the left, my ears will hear a voice behind me, saying, "This is the way; walk in it."

Thank You that Your Scriptures continually reveal You to me.

Judy Anderson
Codirector, Executive & Embassy Ministries
Eastern Europe, Russia

TODAY'S TIP: Have one Bible verse fixed in your mind as you go into treatments, and concentrate on that.

PRAYER REFERENCES: Hebrews 4:12–13; 2 Timothy 3:15–17; Psalm 119:105; Isaiah 30:19–21

Fixing My Thoughts on God

You will keep in perfect peace all who trust in you,
whose thoughts are fixed on you! Trust in the
LORD always, for the LORD GOD is the eternal Rock.
—ISAIAH 26:3–4 NLT

After my second dose of chemotherapy, I noticed my brain getting fuzzy. I'd always been able to think through things logically, but now I couldn't focus on anything for long. Simple arithmetic befuddled me; the numbers just wouldn't line up. My brain cleared after a few days, but it didn't return to its former sharpness until well after my treatments were over.

I felt betrayed by my brain. I'd already lost my health. Was even my ability to think clearly being taken away from me? That's when something Elisabeth Elliot wrote in *A Path Through Suffering* leapt off the page at me: "Open hands should characterize the soul's attitude toward God—open to receive what He wants to give, open to give back what He wants to take."[14]

Are my hands open? I thought. *Or are they holding on to the way I want my life to be going?* So I lifted my clenched fists to God and one by one peeled back the fingers until my palms lay open before Him.

Father God, this cancer path has resulted in so many losses. Now I even seem to be losing my ability to think. I'm scared, Lord. I need Your peace. You've promised Your peace to those who trust in You. I want your way, Lord, for I know that You love me and have a plan for my life that is far better than anything I could think up for myself. I choose to trust You, for You, Lord God, are the eternal Rock.

Thank You for loving me enough to die for me. Now I want to die to my preconceived notions of what my life should be like. I choose to follow You wherever You lead me, even if it means the loss of things and abilities I hold dear. I don't want to trust in those abilities, Lord; I want to trust in You. Help me to see those abilities as gifts from You in the first place.

I lift my hands up to You with open palms—they are empty of my plans and are ready to receive Yours. Transform me into the person You want me to be.

Amy Givler, MD
Author, *Hope in the Face of Cancer:*
A Survival Guide for the Journey You Did Not Choose

TODAY'S TIP: Lift your clenched fists to God. Then slowly open your hands and tell Him you're ready to let go and ready for Him to fill them.

PRAYER REFERENCE: Isaiah 26:3–4

Not "Why?" but "How?"

*Now to him who is able to do immeasurably
more than all we ask or imagine . . .*
—EPHESIANS 3:20

Twenty years ago, in my first battle with cancer, I came to love the story of Gideon in Judges 6. God told Gideon to raise up an army to fight the Midianites. After needing much confirmation, Gideon gathered close to forty thousand men. Then God told him there were too many! The ranks were narrowed until only three hundred men remained. The Lord then explained that He was keeping the army small so that the Israelites would not boast in their own strength but would know that the Lord saved them.

Do you take enough risk in your own life to know that it is not you, but God who won the battle? I have come to realize that when we step out in faith (or are pushed out, as is the case with cancer!) we begin to see God do extraordinary things. Instead of asking, "Why, Lord?" we need to begin asking, "How, Lord?" "How are you going to work through this? How are you going to provide? I have found that by simply changing the question, my doubt is replaced by the anticipation of seeing how God will do it.

Mighty God, You are able to do immeasurably more than all I ask or imagine according to Your power at work in me. How grateful I am it is not up to me or my strength. Instead, it is Your power at work, the same power that created the universe and holds it together. Nothing is too difficult for You.

I confess that I have asked a lot of "whys" instead of trusting You with how You will use what I am going through. I praise You because You have a plan far greater than I can imagine. In faith, I thank You for placing me here so that I can experience Your provision and Your love. I praise You that out of Your glorious riches You will strengthen me with power through Your Spirit in my inner being. This is the same power that raised Jesus from the dead and seated Him at the right hand in the heavenly realms. Now that's power!

Lord, I come humbly before Your throne, asking, "How?" How will You . . .? [Take a few moments to rephrase some of your "why" questions.] Thank You that I can trust You with these needs. I look forward to seeing how You do it.

Susan Sorensen

TODAY'S TIP: Write out some questions for God that begin with "How?"

PRAYER REFERENCES: Ephesians 3:20; Ephesians 3:16; Colossians 1:17; Ephesians 1:19

The Balm of Gilead

*We are afflicted in every way, but not crushed . . .
always carrying in the body the death of Jesus, so that
the life of Jesus may also be made visible in our bodies.*
—2 CORINTHIANS 4:8–10 NRSV

It was my second session of chemotherapy, and my body was beginning to wear down. I knew that my hair would soon fall out. As I showered, it felt like ants crawling over my scalp as hair began to clog the drain. I had always been grateful for my nice, easy-to-manage platinum blond hair.

As I washed the hair away, I began to feel like weeping. Yet in that same instant, I felt a warm sense of love overflowing in my body. It was as if the Savior was saying, *As you let go of what is precious to you, so My love is washing any remains of cancer down the drain. Learn to rely on Me. I am your source.*

Then the words of Henri Nouwen echoed back to me: "Let this time of tiredness be a time of solitude where you can recharge your life, where your wounds are oiled by the balm of Gilead, your muscles massaged, your courage renewed, and your body nourished by my love."[15] I began to learn to let go and let God wash, renew, and produce new growth in my life.

The Balm of Gilead

I praise You, Lord God. In Your great mercy You have given me new birth into a living hope through the resurrection of Jesus Christ from the dead. You have also given me an inheritance that can never perish, spoil, or fade—kept in heaven for me. In this I greatly rejoice! Though now I may have to suffer grief through trials. This has come so that my faith—of greater worth than gold—may be proved genuine and may result in praise, glory, and honor when Jesus Christ is revealed.

Even as I experience losses in life, I see this as a new beginning of drawing close to the feet of Christ. Help me endure the pain with expectancy toward the promise of Your perfecting work in me. Give me the stamina I need for today and the courage to face tomorrow. I open my mind and spirit to Your divine love and direction.

Joyce Van Dyk
Minister and chaplain

TODAY'S TIP: Visualize your body being renewed by God as cancer strips away some of your physical attributes.

PRAYER REFERENCE: 1 Peter 1:1–7

Counting on
His Faithfulness

The steadfast love of the LORD never ceases,
his mercies never come to an end; they are
new every morning; great is thy faithfulness.
—LAMENTATIONS 3:22–23 RSV

During my cancer journey, there were times I felt strong in the Lord and at peace. At other times, I was overcome with fear. There were times when I felt too weak to pray the simplest prayer and times when I felt less surrendered to the will of God than ever before. Yet never did I experience His turning away. Rather, I had a heightened awareness of His tenderness as He reminded me of verses like Isaiah 42:3: "A bruised reed he will not break, and a smoldering wick he will not snuff out."

One night in the hospital, during a recurrence of the cancer, I couldn't sleep. I kept saying Bible verses over and over, trying to cast my cares on Him, but peace and rest would not come. In the middle of the night, a female resident doctor, whom I had never seen and have never seen since, came to my bedside. She asked if I wanted her to pray for me. Then she prayed as one who knew the Lord, and when she left I fell asleep.

God had sent a woman of faith to give me a sense of His presence, to lift me before the Lord when my own faith was faltering. Great is His faithfulness!

O faithful and mighty God, how limitless are Your mercies, how steadfast is Your love. You never grow weary, You never waiver, and You never change. Your power and compassion are never diminished by time or circumstances or by the number of prayers You answer.

Thank You for hiding me in Your shelter in the day of trouble, for surrounding me with people of Your choosing to pray for me, to encourage me, and to lift me before You when I feel too weak to call upon You myself. You have made these dear ones part of the shelter You provide for me.

I praise You for Your unfailing faithfulness—a faithfulness that does not depend on my faithfulness to You, a faithfulness that assures me that You will not allow anything to come to me that has not first passed through Your mighty yet tender hands, a faithfulness that enables me to rest securely in Your everlasting arms.

Melinda Merwin
Homemaker

TODAY'S TIP: Thank God for the ways He has shown His faithfulness to you.

PRAYER REFERENCES: Lamentations 3:22–23; Psalm 91:1; 1 Corinthians 1:9

The Woman in the Mirror

59

Do you not know that you are the temple of
God and that the Spirit of God dwells in you?
—1 CORINTHIANS 3:16 NKJV

During the course of chemotherapy treatments, my body changed. I was very thin with a few sprigs of hair sticking out of my scalp. My skin was a pasty white, and even though I slept *a lot*, I had dark circles under my eyes.

I share this with you not to discourage you but to let you know that you're not alone if you are wondering who that woman in the mirror really is. The good news? I quickly gained back weight and lots of hair, and although I don't sleep nearly as much now, I don't have circles under my eyes any-more—maybe just a few more wrinkles!

But I came to understand that my body and mind, although crucial to my survival on earth, were not the essence of who I was then or who I am today. I came from God and will return to Him when my time here is done. With that knowledge, cancer lost much of its grip on me. It could never have the "real me." That part was already taken. It had been bought and paid for on the cross of Calvary.

Lord Jesus, thank You for promising to renew me day by day. I confess that it is difficult to look so different, to feel so weak, to have life change so abruptly. I'm glad I have You to remind me of what really matters. You make this bearable. You did not promise an easy life, but You did promise to be with me when challenges come. I need You now, Lord. Thank You for being here and helping me to face the changes that are happening. They are only temporary, but You are eternal.

I thank You that You chose to make my body Your temple—that Your Spirit lives in me. I have been hard pressed on every side but not crushed; perplexed but not abandoned; struck down but not destroyed. I praise You that these light and momentary troubles are achieving an eternal glory!

Pam Brown
Author, *Facing Cancer Together*

TODAY'S TIP: Do something that renews you: take a scented bath, get a hand and foot massage, visit a special friend . . . or take a nap.

PRAYER REFERENCES: 1 Corinthians 3:16; 2 Corinthians 4:7–10, 17

A Very Special Birthday

These things I have spoken to you,
that my joy may be in you, and
that your joy may be made full.

—JOHN 15:11 NASB

It was my forty-eighth birthday, and I always like to do something special on my birthday. Having lived through cancer myself, I knew exactly how I wanted to celebrate. My dear friend Lorraine was due for a chemotherapy treatment. I wanted to be with her and asked if I could come along and sit with her during the six-hour ordeal.

Lorraine already had the IV in her arm when I arrived. She was smiling big when I walked in, and I felt like sobbing. How could she have so much joy at a time like this?

We visited with each other like we were on a date for high tea. Then all of a sudden, she pulled out a bag with her "free" arm and started taking out party favors and goodies—even a picnic to celebrate my birthday. Can you imagine?

Needless to say, Lorraine is my hero for life! She was living in her *faith*, not in her *feelings*, for sure. By the way, after her treatments ended, Lorraine and her husband went twice to

Russia and adopted two little orphans to add to their family. Cancer is not for wimps!

You are the Father of campassion and the God of all comfort. You comfort me in all my troubles so that I can comfort those in trouble with the comfort I have received from You. For just as the sufferings of Christ flow over into my life, so also, through Christ, my comfort overflows.

Father, thank You for Your compassion and comfort. You alone give joy in the midst of pain and suffering. How grateful I am that You even desire to place Your joy in me—and that You desire that my joy may be made full. Your power is truly perfected in my weakness. I praise You that Your promises remain true to me no matter what I am going through. You know my future and my past. I am thankful I don't need to be afraid, because You go with me, and you will never leave me nor forsake me. You give me life and breath, and every day is Your gift to me. Thank You, Jesus.

Debbie Petersen
Women of Faith Conference staff

TODAY'S TIP: Find a reason to celebrate and do it.
PRAYER REFERENCES: 2 Corinthians 1:3–5, John 15:11, Hebrews 13:5–6

An Unexpected Gift

61

*Moses' arms finally became too tired
to hold up the staff any longer. So
Aaron and Hur found a stone for him
to sit on. Then they stood on each side,
holding up his hands until sunset.*

—EXODUS 17:12 NLT

My family was overwhelmed by the goodness of the people as I went through surgeries, chemotherapy, and radiation. Yet one act of kindness will always stand out to remind me that God cares about our everyday needs and desires.

David, my eleven-year-old son, asked me if I could bake some sweet rolls. After all, it had been a long time since Mom had done any baking. I hardly had the energy to leave my bedroom, and the smell of food nauseated me. How could I fulfill this request? David was understanding but disappointed.

Late that evening, David answered a knock at our door. He was greeted by a neighbor holding a box of freshly baked cinnamon rolls. She said, "I thought your family might enjoy these." I will forever treasure the memory of his smile and be grateful that God cared about a young boy's request.

An Unexpected Gift

Lord, You comprehend my path and my lying down, and You are acquainted with all my ways. There is not a word on my tongue that You do not know. You provide in ways I can't even imagine.

How grateful I am for Your promise to supply all my needs according to Your riches in glory by Christ Jesus. I believe You have shown Yourself through the people who have surrounded me during this weary time. Thank You for those who have come alongside and lifted my arms. I am grateful that You often use servants who listen to Your voice to be Your hands and Your feet.

You, Lord Jesus, are the friend who sticks closer than a brother. You are always true and faithful. I worship You. I trust all to You. I accept Your peace and grace.

Sue Stalzer
Homemaker and teacher

TODAY'S TIP: At times you will have no energy. Let friends know of your needs.

PRAYER REFERENCES: Psalm 139:3–4; Luke 12:29–31; Philippians 4:19; Proverbs 18:24

Closet Time

62

O LORD, You have searched me and known me.
You know my sitting down and my rising up;
You understand my thought afar off.
—PSALM 139:1–2 NKJV

One Sunday after my first chemotherapy treatment, I was unable to go with my family to church because my cell counts were too low. My husband, Gordy, leafed through our very disorganized front hall closet to find his gloves. Hats and scarves tumbled to the ground. After breakfast, I vowed to go through the dreaded pigsty.

I took everything out of the closet and began to sort into the usual keep and discard piles. As I surveyed the contents, I was surprised to see items I had forgotten about. Some were valuable but hidden under the disorganization. Other items were taking up valuable space. I eventually developed a third pile to ask Gordy and the kids about.

As I leafed through the mess, I thought about how God was using cancer to clean out the closets of my own life. He was forcing me to discard unneeded things like busyness and pride. God was looking at what didn't fit and also showing me some buried "gems." Cleaning out my coat closet began a much-needed evaluation of my life!

O Lord, You know everything about me and have forgiven me even when I fail You and cling to things that don't last. I praise You for exposing the condition of my closets through this trial and helping me clean them out. How grateful I am that You care more for the condition of my heart than my activities. I certainly see many things in my life going up like hay and stubble in the flames of this trial. It's not easy being refined through fire, but I'm grateful for the promise of an end result that brings You glory.

I praise You for being the Master Builder. Unless You build the house, I labor in vain to build it. Thank you for working out your good plan in my life. Thank You for forcing me to build on a Rock and not on needless things that sink because of a sandy foundation.

You have hedged me in behind and before. You have laid Your hand on me. Such knowledge is too wonderful for me. I praise You!

Laura Geist

TODAY'S TIP: Clean out a closet in your home, and take a moment to ask God about any housecleaning He needs to do in your life.

PRAYER REFERENCES: Isaiah 48:10; Psalm 127:1; Matthew 7:24–27; Psalm 139:5

The Best Prescription of All

*Do not be anxious about anything, but in
everything, by prayer and petition, with
thanksgiving, present your requests to God.*

—PHILIPPIANS 4:6

I've filled a lot of prescriptions in my life, but the best prescription of all came not from my doctor but from God. Our Lord has given us a simple prescription for anxiety—pray. This medication claims to bring the peace of God that transcends all understanding. That is a big claim for a simple solution to emotional anguish and pain. Yet God made it simple. He says to "pray . . . with thanksgiving" and "present your requests" about whatever is making you anxious. He then promises to give us peace and guard our hearts and minds in Christ Jesus.

In John Bunyan's classic allegory *Pilgrim's Progress*, Christian comes to the cross and unloads the heavy burden he's been carrying on his back. God gives us the opportunity to do the same thing! Psalm 147:11 says, "His joy is in those who reverence him, those who expect him to be loving and kind" (TLB). I love this!

When we don't entrust our cares to Him, we are saying,

in essence, "I don't trust You to be loving and kind." We need to confess this lack of faith and then lay our burdens at His feet. "Cast all your anxiety on him because he cares for you" (1 Peter 5:7).

I praise You, Lord, at all times. Even when I feel afflicted, You are near. Thank You for allowing me to seek You and for faithfully answering me when I call on You. You deliver me from all my fears. Those who look to You are never covered with shame. You save me out of all my troubles. Your angels encamp around those who fear You, and You deliver them. You are faithful. I praise You for delivering me from all my fears.

How grateful I am that You gave me the privilege of coming to You and laying my concerns at your feet. You desire that I cast all my cares on You. Right now I lay my greatest anxieties before You . . . [Share the greatest burdens of your heart.]

I praise You for the promise of Your peace, which transcends all understanding and will guard my mind and heart. I rejoice that my anxieties are no longer in my hands but in the same hands that hold the world. You will care for me and for my every need. I praise You!
Susan Sorensen

TODAY'S TIP: Write out your own prescription for anxiety—Philippians 4:6–7—and fill it often!
PRAYER REFERENCES: Psalm 34:1–7; Philippians 4:6–7

His Eye Is on the Sparrow

*Your Father knows what you
need before you ask him.*
—MATTHEW 6:8

On the way to my mailbox, I looked up and saw a bird's nest in our crab apple tree. This was no ordinary nest. Its owner had skillfully woven a ribbon throughout, the tail happily blowing in the wind. The Tiffany-blue ribbon was my favorite color and looked so bright at a point when my future looked so dim. I felt pure delight. God was giving His creatures exactly what they needed. He would provide for me through every need and decision related to my cancer journey —and for life!

God often takes the ordinary events of life and makes a supernatural thing happen that could only be from Him. I felt like God had done this just for me. My emotions were jump-started as I was reminded of His faithfulness and presence with me. That's what the glory of God means. It is an encounter with God's very presence. Because of His incredible love for us, He intends to make Himself known to us and become part of our everyday existence.

Father, You care for the birds of the air and the lilies of the field. You provide for them daily. And You promise to care even more so for me. You tell me not to worry, because You know what I need and You know the specific things that concern me. Thank You, Father.

In You, Lord, I have taken refuge. Keep me safe. Turn Your ear to me and come quickly to my rescue. You are my rock and my fortress. For the sake of Your name, lead and guide me. I trust in You. You are my God and my times are in Your hands. How great is Your goodness, which You have stored up for those who revere You, which You give to those who take refuge in You.

In the shelter of Your presence You hide me. In Your dwelling You keep me safe. Praise be to the Lord, for You show Your wonderful love to me in large and small ways throughout each day!

Connie Hastings
Author, *The Savvy Cook*,
cancer support group coordinator

TODAY'S TIP: As cancer slows life down, take time to see and hear your loving Father.

PRAYER REFERENCES: Matthew 6:8, 26; Psalm 31:1–3, 14–15, 19–21

MRI: Mini Roll Insertion

[The LORD GOD said,] "When my glory passes by,
I will put you in a cleft in the rock and cover
you with my hand until I have passed by."

—EXODUS 33:22

In my book, MRI really stands for Mini Roll Insertion or Magnificent Racket Inducer. The experience made me feel like I was being inserted into the tiny center of a giant roll of bathroom tissue—or, more accurately, the even smaller metal tube of a toilet-tissue holder. Inside the tube, it sounded like a giant drummer was pounding away right above my face.

I came out of my first MRI with a stronger urge to draw nearer to the Father. It started when a friend told me it helps, when you're having any MRI or CAT scan, to have someone hold your feet as you lie inside the tube. It reminds you you're not alone and provides comfort, she said.

I've since had lots of MRIs and CAT scans, and several friends have volunteered to be my foot holders, but I have declined. I've had Someone else helping me. When I'm in that small, confined space, I picture myself hidden away in "a cleft in the rock," covered gently with God's own hand as His magnificent glory thunders by. And in that loud, tight, toilet-paper tube of a place, I feel an unusual sense of comforting peace.[16]

I thank You, Lord, that Your response to Moses is Your response to me: "My presence will go with you, and I will give you rest." What comfort this brings. For in the day of trouble, You will keep me safe in Your dwelling; You will hide me in the shelter of Your tabernacle and set me high upon a rock. Then my head will be exalted above the enemies who surround me. Because of Your daily presence, I experience Your joy. You place me in a cleft in the rock and cover me with Your hand. Thank You for Your gentle care and protection.

Father, I am especially thankful for Your presence in my brokenness. I'm grateful brokenness brings wholeness in a variety of ways. Broken hearts, broken bodies, broken dream—and then, in the midst of my brokenness, I feel myself pressed against the unshakable presence of God. And there I find peace; there I find strength and courage for the next step. There I find You!

Barbara Johnson
Best-selling author, *Plant a Geranium in Your Cranium*

TODAY'S TIP: How do you make God laugh? Tell Him your plans.[17]

PRAYER REFERENCES: Exodus 33:14; Psalm 27:5–6

A Hot Flash
Is Not a News Bulletin

*In my distress I cried unto
the LORD, and he heard me.*

—PSALM 120:1 KJV

A husband of a cancer patient must have patience:

"Open that window wider!"

"Get those covers off of me!"

"Could we have a little air-conditioning, please?"

But if you have been there, you know the next phase, three minutes later:

"Shut that window!"

"I need more covers!"

After a few weeks of chemotherapy, my list of enemies from cancer changed from cancer cells, radiation, and chemotherapy—to cancer cells, menopause, and menopause.

The hot flashes were impossible to anticipate. I could never figure out what triggered them. Once when I was sitting in a chilly lecture hall, I tried to get one to come. I couldn't and nearly froze for an hour. Coworkers got used to me running out the door to breathe in some cold Montana air—only to rush back in and put my sweater on, freezing from the inside out!

Since that time, progress has been made in dealing with chemically induced menopause. My husband says, "Praise the Lord!" Only he knows how awful my emotions tumbled during those months—well, he and me and the Lord. I am thankful God and my husband forgave me for the mood swings. Only by God's grace did we make it through.[18]

Praise You, Lord, for Your grace and mercy. You bring not only physical healing but healing for hurting emotions. My attitudes and bad moods are no surprise to You. You know them, and still You love me. Thank You for Your forgiveness and for those around me who love me despite my moodiness. And when I have succumbed to an emotional outburst, how grateful I am that I need only tell You. I cry out with King David, "Have mercy on me, O God, according to Your loving kindness; according to the multitude of Your tender mercies, blot out my transgressions. Wash me thoroughly from my iniquity, and cleanse me from my sin. Create in me a clean heart, O God, and renew a steadfast spirit within me. Restore to me the joy of Your salvation, and uphold me by Your generous Spirit." Thank You! Praise You!

Lois Olmstead
Author, *Breast Cancer and Me*

TODAY'S TIP: Wear layers. Being prepared and understanding that "this too shall pass" will help you make it through.

PRAYER REFERENCE: Psalm 51:1–2, 10–12

Prayer Is Not a Feeling

*He is a rewarder of those
who diligently seek Him.*

—HEBREWS 11:6 NKJV

This was not like me. I did not feel like praying. In the past, I felt the need to pray and the joy of praying. I daily experienced the privilege of coming to my heavenly Father. I now found myself unable to pray as I wanted. Was it the chemo drugs or a preoccupation with what my future might hold? My prayers were brief and abrupt.

Then one day I recognized my error. I was relying on my feelings! Feelings are not the measure of truth; only the facts found in the Bible are true, perfect, and eternal. And the Bible tells me that God is in control and knows the desires of my heart. My Father welcomes me as His daughter, and He will hear my voice even when I am weak and faltering. Psalm 105:4 says, "Seek the LORD and His strength; seek His face evermore" (NKJV). This instruction is not subject to my feelings.

Gratefully, too, I was made aware of the many gracious people who prayed for me. What a loving provision God made when He put concern for my welfare on the hearts of others.

It still humbles me to remember the sustaining power of those prayers.

Father, I thank You that You hear prayers uttered by individual voices. You are never too busy or unavailable. You have no call waiting. How amazing it is that You, the God of creation, hear me. You are near to all who call on You in truth. Your love reaches to the heavens and Your faithfulness to the skies. O Lord, You preserve me. How priceless is Your unfailing love. I find refuge in You. I rest in Your goodness to me. For You are the fountain of life.

Thank You, Lord, for the gift of Your Son, who is interceding for me. Nothing in all creation can separate me from the love You give me in Jesus my Lord. I believe in the healing power of prayer through Jesus, the Great Physician.

Thank You for those who pray for me. You have placed this desire on their hearts, and I am grateful. Thank You for Your indwelling Holy Spirit, who comforts and intercedes when thoughts don't come easily. Thank You for the privilege and provision of prayer even when my feelings deceive me. I praise You for Your patience with me, my unchanging Lord.

Pam Formsma
Mother and grandmother

TODAY'S TIP: Take a moment to pray for a friend of yours in need of God's comfort and healing.
PRAYER REFERENCES: Psalm 145:18; Psalm 36:5–9; Romans 8:34, 39

Disappointed Plans

But the LORD still waits for you to come
to him so he can show you his love and
compassion. For the LORD is a faithful God.
—ISAIAH 30:18 NLT

After six months of chemotherapy for Hodgkin's lymphoma, I thought I was through. When my oncologist had mapped out his initial plan, I'm sure he warned me that the plan could change. But I hadn't heard it. I hadn't wanted to.

So when he walked into the examining room, I was unprepared to hear, "You need two more months of chemotherapy." My tumor, though tiny, was still shrinking. If a cancer cell or two were still alive, the time to kill them was then. *Two more months.* I was crushed.

That's when I remembered what Corrie ten Boom once said. After suffering in a German concentration camp during World War II, she traveled the world to speak about Jesus, who, despite the darkness of the concentration camp, had never left her. "When the train goes through a dark tunnel and the world gets dark, do you jump out? Of course not. You sit still and trust the engineer to get you through."[19]

So I clung to God, praying He would get me through this dark tunnel of disappointment. I nestled close to my heavenly Father, and He carried me through.

Precious God, You know how overwhelmed I feel right now. I come to You because You have promised to show me Your love and compassion. In fact, You have said that You are waiting for me to come to You. I do come, for how I need to experience Your personal concern and care of me. Great are Your tender mercies, O Lord.

I know that I am Your beloved child and that You—like a loving Father—know exactly what I need. Help me face disappointing news, knowing that You are carrying me. You see the future as clearly as You see the past. I want to see this day as You see it—to see how it fits into Your perfect plan for my life. Give me a glimpse into the purpose for my suffering.

You are a faithful God. Many are the wonders You have done. The things You have planned for me no one can recount to You; were I to speak and tell of them, they would be too many to declare. Not one of Your promises has ever failed. I wait, O Lord, for Your help.

Amy Givler, MD
Author, *Hope in the Face of Cancer:*
A Survival Guide for the Journey You Did Not Choose

TODAY'S TIP: Look around for someone else who is hurting and speak a word of comfort.

PRAYER REFERENCES: Isaiah 30:18; Psalm 40:5

The Whisper of God

The LORD said, "Go out and stand on the mountain in the presence of the LORD . . ." Then a great and powerful wind tore the mountains apart . . . but the LORD was not in the wind . . . there was an earthquake, but the LORD was not in the earthquake . . . a fire, but the LORD was not in the fire. And after the fire came a gentle whisper.

—1 KINGS 19:11–12

Elijah of the Old Testament was a mere human being, one who was privileged to see great manifestations of the power of Almighty God. Therefore, Elijah expected to see God in something bigger than himself when he was told to wait for the presence of the Lord to pass by. He wouldn't have been surprised to encounter God in a powerful wind, a huge earthquake, or a roaring fire. But a gentle whisper? Yes, that's exactly how God came to a depressed and despondent Elijah—in a gentle whisper.

My family ministered to me in a tender and loving way with the "whisper of God" when I was in an induced coma in ICU. They brought a CD player and my favorite instrumental CDs into my hospital room. With the permission of the nurses, the music was played softly, like the whisper of God into my sub-consciousness. After I awoke, I remembered how the words of the old hymns—long ago memorized—had gently ministered to me.

Lord Jesus, open my spiritual ears to "hear" Your gentle whispers of comfort, peace, and assurance. Even though I feel like I'm enduring a tremendous tornado in my life, I know You desire that I simply be still and know that You are God. Thank You for Your promise to sustain me on my sickbed and restore me from my bed of illness. You are faithful!

I am grateful You desire to show Your loving-kindness and gentleness to me. Your very nature is love. And it is out of that love that You are patient with me and all people, not wanting anyone to perish but all to come to repentance, to turn and experience a love relationship with You through Jesus Christ.

Thank You for being patient with me. If I listen with my heart, I can receive grace amazingly given in just the right portion for my present need. Father God, it is indeed a delight to trust in You.

Betty Jo Lewis
Prayer warrior

TODAY'S TIP: Listen to the whisper of God in music that adores and magnifies Him.

PRAYER REFERENCES: 1 Kings 19:11–12; Psalm 46:10; Psalm 41:3; 2 Peter 3:9

The Fruit of Suffering

Consider it pure joy, my brothers, whenever you face trials of many kinds, because you know that the testing of your faith develops perseverance. Perseverance must finish its work so that you may be mature and complete, not lacking in anything.

—JAMES 1:2–4 ASV

According to a footnote in my Bible, God has eight purposes for suffering: to produce fruit, to silence the devil, to glorify God, to make us more like Jesus, to teach us dependence, to refine our lives, to rebuke sin, and to enlarge our ministry.

Of all of these purposes, God gave me a strong desire to "enlarge my ministry." Each time I went to the hospital, I found opportunities to tell others about Him. The Lord opened doors in waiting rooms with other patients and with technicians when I'd ask about their lives and prayer needs. People were amazingly open and appreciative that someone would even ask about them, for example, the young parking attendant who would run to park my car because I showed an interest in him and his reason for coming to this country. On my last day of radiation, I gave him a Bible in his native language, which he eagerly received.

When I was first diagnosed, I decided that no matter the outcome, God would be glorified. I wanted to be used through this experience to tell others where my hope lay—in Jesus!

Lord, Your hands made me and formed me. May those who know You rejoice when they see me, for I have put my hope in You, my Creator. You are perfect, and in faithfulness You have allowed me to go through this challenging time. May Your unfailing love be my comfort. Let Your compassion come to me daily that I may live to glorify You.

I praise You for the work You do through suffering. Help me rest in Your perfect plan and allow You to use me. Open up doors of opportunity to tell others about You. I feel so inadequate in this, but I know I can trust You to give me the words to say in every situation. You have promised that at the needed time You will give me what to say, for it will be Your Spirit speaking through me.

I praise You for the overflow of Your goodness in me that touches others' lives. How can I repay You for all Your goodness to me? I will tell others of Your love and faithfulness as I call on Your name.

Kay Luther
Homemaker

TODAY'S TIP: Consider what purpose the Lord may have for your suffering and how He may use you through it.

PRAYER REFERENCES: Psalm 119:73–77; Matthew 10:19–20; Psalm 116:12–13

Surrendered

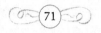

Your will be done on earth as it is in heaven.
—MATTHEW 6:10

It was the day I would find out if the cancer was growing or shrinking. I put on the hospital robe and stood shivering in the bathroom (the shivers being a combination of fear and cold). I looked at myself in the mirror and felt driven to my knees, a very familiar place, especially during the past few months.

As I began praying, the shivers stopped. I talked to God about the desires of my heart. He knew what they were—I wanted to live. I had been asking Him to heal me for months now. But even more than wanting to live, I *really* wanted my will to be His will, even if it meant that my time on earth was almost up. I knew that God would be with me, no matter what the results of the CAT scan were.

I was grateful for every bit of God's gift of life, no matter how long or short it was. The God who loved me and had taken such good care of me would continue to do so should cancer march through my body. It was at that point I knew my prayers had been answered, for my surrendered heart experienced God's peace that is beyond understanding.

Lord, I thank You for my life. You know the desires of my heart, and I lift them up to you now. I pray for . . . [Share specific desires of your heart.]

How grateful I am that I can surrender my desires into Your loving care. I am so thankful I can rest secure in the fact that You are faithful. You tell me to cast my cares and anxiety on You because You care for me. Great is Your love, Lord, higher than the heavens. Your faithfulness reaches to the skies. Be exalted, O God, above the heavens, and let Your glory be over all the earth.

Be glorified in my life as well. I really want my will to be Your will. Grow me up this day so that my will is molded into Yours. Whatever You have in store for me, give me the strength to accept it and to glorify You every step of the way. You truly do understand my hurts, my fears, my pains as You made the ultimate sacrifice for me. Thank You for guarding my heart and my mind with Your peace.

Pam Brown

Author, *Facing Cancer Together*

TODAY'S TIP: Start a prayer journal. Write down your prayer requests and watch God work!

PRAYER REFERENCES: 1 Peter 5:7; Psalm 108:1–5; Matthew 6:10

Forever Blooming

*All men are like grass, and all their glory is like
the flowers of the field . . . The grass withers and the
flowers fall, but the word of our God stands forever.*

—ISAIAH 40:6–8

I love flowers and can spend countless hours tending to my
garden. I pull weeds, prune shrubs, and plant seasonal flowers. I fertilize, mulch, and water. Then, in a short period of
time, everything needs to be done again.

During my treatments related to breast cancer, I watched
from my bedroom window as my friends tended to my garden.
They came by daily all summer long to weed and water, and
they even planted one hundred caladium bulbs for me to enjoy.

It was not until I was unable to keep my yard in tip-top
shape myself that I began to understand what really matters.
God used the flowers (which would not last forever) to help
me realize I needed to concentrate on the three things that are
everlasting: God, His Word, and the souls of people. God used
my friends as the messengers of His Word to show the way to
eternal life for our souls after our bodies wither away. And I
began to focus on those things that are forever blooming.

O Lord, You have given me only a short life on this earth when compared to eternity. My lifetime is like nothing to You. Everyone's life is only a breath. So, Lord, what hope do I have? You are my hope! I praise You that You are with me now and will be with me throughout eternity. I praise You for Your promise this day that I am blessed when I persevere under trials. How grateful I am that when I have withstood the test I will receive the crown of life that You have promised to those who love You.

Thank You for Your grace and Your healing touch. Thank You for helping me see beyond temporary things, as pleasing as they may be, and put my eyes on Your eternal glory. This life is not about me, but sometimes I feel like it is. Help me remember that this body, whether healthy or sick, will last only a short while. I want to give myself to You and those things that will last forever. All to Your glory!

Donna Lewis
Interior decorator,
CanCare board member

〰 TODAY'S TIP: Let the temporary things be just that. Concentrate on God's words of love, for they will bloom forever in your heart.

〰 PRAYER REFERENCES: Psalm 39:5, 7; James 1:12; Isaiah 40:6–8

Deep Beauty

*So the King will greatly desire
your beauty; because He
is your LORD, worship Him.*
—PSALM 45:11 NKJV

Some days I don't like to look in the mirror. My once smooth skin shows the scars of eight different breast surgeries. My hair must be colored back to its original auburn hue and chemically treated to combat the post-chemo frizziness. Some days I feel far from a natural beauty! Fortunately, God sees beyond the war wounds of cancer. He looks at my heart. When He sees me surrender myself to Him and begin to love His Word, I am the prettiest girl in the room!

It is interesting to consider that Jesus did not come to this earth as a handsome or wealthy man to attract people. Instead, He humbled himself to die on a cross and remove our sin so that we could be made gorgeous women—flaws and all—in God's sight. His wounds on the cross (they weren't pretty!) made us right and beautiful before God.

When I look at the remnants of cancer on my own body, I am reminded that there is a deeper beauty, one I can't manufacture, but one God can produce when I give my heart to Him.

Lord, how grateful I am that You do not look at the things man looks at. Man looks at the outward appearance, but You look at the heart. I praise You for not only looking at my heart but choosing to clean it up and make it beautiful because of Jesus's sacrifice on the cross. Lord, thank You for being willing to be afflicted on my behalf so that I could be made perfect in Your sight. Thank You for being willing to be physically scarred so that I could be beautiful before the King of the universe.

Help me to focus not on what cancer is doing to my physical body, but how You are making and molding the inside of me. I thank You for this opportunity to shine because of Your perfect work in me, a work far more important and lasting than my physical appearance. I praise You for the promise that those who look to You are radiant; their faces are never covered with shame. Fill me to overflowing with Your radiance and light!

Laura Geist

TODAY'S TIP: As you look in the mirror at what cancer has left behind, be thankful to the Lord for exchanging His scars for your beauty.

PRAYER REFERENCES: 1 Samuel 16:7; Isaiah 53:4; Psalm 34:5

Humor Saved the Day!

The joy of the LORD is your strength.
—NEHEMIAH 8:10 NKJV

Oh, she's the family zombie," my eldest daughter would say as I wandered away from a conversation or through a room. Chemo had made my mind so restless I couldn't carry on a normal conversation. Thankfully, the change was only temporary.

How does a family cope when Mom is so abnormal? For our family, Amy's humor saved the day! The wise adage, "If you can't change a situation, adjust and move on" seemed to be a good tactic. My oncologist explained that the aggressive cancer had to be dealt with in the most *aggressive* manner. There were no two ways about it. In the stress of the valley, we had to remember to practice a joyful heart. There wasn't joy in my poor mind, but humor helped me remember to be strong through joy.

Even in adverse circumstances, Nehemiah found his strength in delighting in the Lord and encouraged others to do the same. He motivated them to pass this enthusiasm on to others. It was important for me to give others the *right* to be happy even when I wasn't.

Heavenly Father, You are my hiding place. You preserve me through difficult times. You surround me with songs of hope. I know that my future is in Your hands. You know what's best for me and my loved ones. I thank You for how You have brought about healing and for Your peace that passes all understanding and guards my heart and mind through Christ Jesus.

Even though there has been much weeping, I know that You have said, "Weeping may endure for a night, but joy comes in the morning." Thank You for all the joy You have brought through family and friends. Thank You for all the healing that comes from visits. It pulls me through. I have felt Your presence in their loving care. I ask that You always make me hear joy and gladness even when it seems humanly impossible. You have said, "A cheerful heart is good medicine." I want Your good medicine to flow through me and produce a cheerful heart. Thank You!

Eva Rice
Retired office worker, former public speaker

☙ TODAY'S TIP: Laugh at everything that you can. You'll feel better, and so will others around you!
☙ PRAYER REFERENCES: Psalm 32:7; Psalm 31:15; Philippians 4:7; Psalm 30:5; Proverbs 17:22

Can I Exchange
This Tent for Another?

*Enlarge the place of your tent, stretch your
tent curtains wide, do not hold back.*

—Isaiah 54:2

This earthly tent has been cut, sewn, patched up, and repaired. I often wish I could exchange it for a newer one! But God's ways are not my ways. He takes the weak things and makes them strong. In my limitations, God's plan and power are limitless.

I'm learning to get my eyes off the tent and onto how to enlarge it. God is able to do wonderful things in and through my life. Instead of being overwhelmed by the imperfections of my body, I have the privilege and opportunity of watching God work in ways beyond my understanding!

It is true that this temporary shell was not designed to last forever. "The body that is sown is perishable, it is raised imperishable; it is sown in dishonor, it is raised in glory; it is sown in weakness, it is raised in power; it is sown a natural body, it is raised a spiritual body" (1 Corinthians 15:42–44).

I think the Lord would have me long for my heavenly home. And in the meantime, He will keep using this patched-up tent!

Thank You, Lord, for this earthly tent. Forgive me for complaining about it. I am grateful that it is not the one I will have for eternity. You will give me a perfect body then.

I praise You for holding this earthly body in Your hands and guiding all that touches it. You delight in me, not my body. You look at the heart. It is awesome for me to consider that I am the apple of Your eye—that I am special to You. Thank You for loving me.

Enlarge the place of my tent, and stretch my curtains wide. Use this experience for Your glory in ways that I cannot even conceive. I praise You for the new things You are beginning to do. As they spring up, help me to perceive them. You are making a way in the desert and streams in the wasteland. I lay my imperfections and fears at Your feet and ask You to work despite them. You are able to do exceedingly abundantly beyond all I ask or imagine according to Your power that is at work within me.

Susan Sorensen

TODAY'S TIP: Consider the ways God may be enlarging your tent.

PRAYER REFERENCES: Isaiah 54:2; Isaiah 43:19; Ephesians 3:20

My Ebenezer

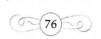

Thus far has the LORD helped us.
—1 SAMUEL 7:12

On my last day of radiation, my husband surprised me with a beautiful ring. We had just been reading in 1 Samuel about the stone that Samuel had set up as a reminder of God's help, and so my ring became for me my Ebenezer, my stone of remembrance.

Little did I know how vital this reminder of God's faithfulness would become. In the year following my treatment, I found myself battling depression. Why in the world would God bring me through cancer in such incredible ways only for me to find it difficult to get out of bed each morning?

I would have repeated my cancer treatments again if it meant I could be spared from this black hole. Yet if depression meant I continued to seek the Lord as I had during treatments, then perhaps this, too, could be redeemed.

I began to watch for the word *hope* in the Bible. Surely, God offered me hope in the midst of what felt like hopelessness. As I read I was reminded again and again of His love. Indeed, if I made my bed in hell, I was assured that He would be with me! (Psalm 139:8).

Lord, hear my prayer. Listen to my cry for mercy. In Your faithfulness and righteousness, come to my relief. Forgive me, Lord, for doubting Your goodness. Forgive me for failing to find the beauty and joy in each day that You give. And forgive me for succumbing to hopelessness when You are the God of hope.

I praise You for Your faithfulness and love even when I feel unlovable. When I am sinking into depression, help me call to mind Your promises. It is only because of Your great love that I am not consumed, for Your compassions never fail. They are new every morning. Great is Your faithfulness! You are my portion; therefore I will wait for You.

Answer me quickly, O Lord; my spirit fails. Do not hide Your face from me. Let the morning bring me word of Your unfailing love, for I have put my trust in You. Show me the way I should go, for to You I lift up my soul.

Elizabeth Jane
Homemaker

TODAY'S TIP: Watch for the word *hope* as you read God's Word, and note how often it occurs.

PRAYER REFERENCES: Psalm 143:1; Lamentations 3:21–24; Psalm 143:7–8

No Excuses

*Do not fear, for I am with you; do not
be dismayed, for I am your God. I will
strengthen you and help you; I will
uphold you with my righteous right hand.*

—ISAIAH 41:10

Just one chemo treatment left. Fear quietly became my companion as the day approached—not the fear of dying from breast cancer, but the fear of life beyond it. I was dreading the end of the sessions, not because I enjoyed being fatigued, nauseated, and overweight. Rather, I'd have nothing left to hide behind once I was deemed healthy. That scared me.

Being treated for cancer afforded me a sort of protection. Expectations were lower. People were kinder. Now I would be accountable for my job performance, my level of activity, my weight, and my responses to people. How would I fare without the familiar, comfortable armor?

On my way to the mailbox, I watched my young neighbor careening up the street on his small bicycle, without the familiar training wheels, his father jogging along within arm's reach. The little boy rode fearlessly, confident that what he lacked in balance and skill, his dad could compensate for perfectly. And I knew then that it was time for me to take off my "training wheels" and see how fast my Father could run.

Father, You give strength to the weary, and to him who lacks might You increase power. You have graciously promised to help, protect, and save me. You have given Your name as a strong tower to which I can run and be safe. Cover me with Your arms and encourage me with Your love. Breathe courage into my timid soul that I might live my life to honor You.

You simply desire that I trust in You and do good, dwell in the land and enjoy safe pasture. You tell me to delight myself in You and You will give me the desires of my heart. Help me be content with just that. Help my focus to rest on trusting You, doing good, dwelling, enjoying life—and delighting in You.

Let me rest in Your strength, walk in Your grace, and rejoice in Your faithfulness. Thank You for never changing, for remaining my rock, my fortress, and my redeemer. When I am afraid, I will trust in You, O God, my king, whom I praise.

Joanne Arentson
Wife, mom of three teenagers,
women's ministry director

∽ TODAY'S TIP: Prepare for "reentry." Enlist others' help to create a realistic schedule and routine.

∽ PRAYER REFERENCE: Psalm 37:3–4

God's Woman
in God's Time

*Who knows whether you have come to
the kingdom for such a time as this?*
—ESTHER 4:14 NKJV

The story of Esther is a moving account of an orphaned Jewish girl whose beauty catches the eye of the Persian king. Since Jews were not highly favored in Persia, Esther keeps her heritage a secret as she becomes the new queen. But when the king's evil chieftain, Haman, vows to destroy her kinsmen, Esther wisely intervenes. She risks her own life by going before the king and identifying herself with a doomed people. She is God's woman in the right place at the right time.

We, too, are God's women in the right place at the right time. We may struggle with God's plan, and we are given a choice to look at cancer as a burden or as an opportunity. We can say, "Why me, Lord?" or we can say, "Use me, Lord!"

Esther could have fretted about the fate of her people. Instead, she knew God had appointed her time as queen to save them. We have a real opportunity to tell others about what He is doing in our lives. God has put us on a stage with a much greater purpose than we can imagine!

Lord, You assure me that You know the plans You have for me—plans to prosper me and not to harm me, plans to give me a hope and a future. In faith, I thank You that I am the right woman in the right place at the right time and that You will use me for Your glory.

Lord, thank You for the opportunities You have given me through cancer to testify about Your great power in my life. When I am tempted to wallow in a pity party, turn my eyes from myself to You and Your plan. When I don't feel I have the strength to do this, Lord, graciously lift me up out of the pit, out of the mud and mire, and set my feet on a rock and give me a firm place to stand. Many will see and fear and put their trust in You.

As I struggle through this process, let my life be a beacon of Your light to others. Use me, Lord, to do great things in Your name.

Laura Geist

TODAY'S TIP: Be quick to share how God has worked in your life through your cancer journey.

PRAYER REFERENCES: Jeremiah 29:11; Psalm 40:2–3; Matthew 5:16

Surprise Treasures

*[God] will be the sure foundation for your times, a
rich store of salvation and wisdom and knowledge;
the fear of the LORD is the key to this treasure.*

—ISAIAH 33:6

God is awesome! Through my breast cancer, my husband saw God's faithful hand of guidance and provision. We experienced the unexplainable peace that comes from leaning with all our weight on Him. So when my husband received a diagnosis of stage-four leukemia, he was totally ready to allow God to be in control and lead him.

What an incredible blessing and joy to our lives and marriage this journey has been. As we have depended on God, we have grown so much closer to each other and have enjoyed a depth of love we never dreamed possible.

Along the way He has given us a family, a fellowship of believers who study the Bible with us and pray for us. They hold us up. We are encouraged through their lives. We have met so many precious people—nurses, doctors, patients. Truly our cup overflows. God is so good. *All* His ways contain the riches of His treasures.

Surprise Treasures

You are the treasure above all treasures. You are a sure foundation and rich storehouse of salvation, wisdom, and knowledge. How grateful I am for Your incredible gift—that through Jesus You have reconciled Your creation to Yourself. You give me the privilege of being adopted as Your child and receiving the gift of eternal life.

Thank You for Your promise that I do not lack any spiritual gift as I walk through life's trials. You will keep me strong to the end, so that I will be blameless when You return. You are faithful. Just as You gave a command to the skies and opened the doors of heaven to provide manna for Your people in the desert, You are able to give a command and provide all I need. I am in awe—it takes only a word from You and it is done.

Thank You, God, for setting me free from having to understand —for teaching me to trust in and lean on You with all my heart. I love being nestled in Your arms. I rest securely in Your love. Thank You for the joy of the journey of life in You.

Ruth Ann Dusek
Homemaker

TODAY'S TIP: Treasure God's gifts no matter the appearance of the package.

PRAYER REFERENCES: Isaiah 33:6; 1 Corinthians 1:7–9; Psalm 78:23

Strong Roots

So then, just as you received Christ Jesus as Lord, continue to live in him, rooted and built up in him, strengthened in the faith as you were taught, and overflowing with thankfulness.

—COLOSSIANS 2:6–7

I remember the big, hard maple tree at my grandparents' house. This magnificent tree spoke of power, beauty, age, and deep, deep roots. Most of all, it told of suffering and change through its massive features.

Painted spots on the trunk had mended cracks and sealed off where big limbs once grew. In some harsh moment, this tree experienced disaster as holes were evident on its south side, forcing it to live its years without beautiful symmetry. A huge chain was wrapped around its massive trunk to keep a crack from getting larger. Distorted and rugged, unyielding in every wind, and deeply rooted, it held and stood to greet each season with dignity.

The memory of this tree comforts and encourages me. It seems to call to me and say, "If I can stand and grow through adversity because I felt loved and nourished, you, too, can gather nourishment from your roots to stand tall among life's challenging moments . . . even cancer."

Lord, I am grateful that You are not looking for perfection, but for trust and dependence. You desire that I do the best I can do each day, supplied by my roots in You. That's enough. That's the key to knowing beauty and strength and feeling completely loved and content.

When I gaze on Your glory, my imperfections become completely irrelevant. Your grace is transforming. I look in the mirror and see healing deeper than the skin, all the way to my heart and spirit. When I walk hand in hand with You, I feel Your love and mercy. You make me strong and mended, to go out into the world as a valuable child of Yours. It is You, Lord, who has held me together, patching holes and mending cracks.

Thank You for making me like a tree planted by streams of water, which yields its fruit in season. My leaf does not wither. Whatever I do I will prosper—all because my roots are in You!

Laurann Patterson
Homemaker and retired teacher

༄ TODAY'S TIP: Bring your imperfections to the Lord, and experience His transforming grace.

༄ PRAYER REFERENCES: Colossians 2:6–7; Psalm 1:3

Now Where Did I Put It?

I will greatly rejoice in the LORD,
my soul shall be joyful in my
God; for he hath clothed me
with the garments of salvation.

—ISAIAH 61:10 KJV

Even before chemotherapy, I sometimes lacked concentration. One day I went to the laundry room and prepared to do my washing. I started the water in the machine and then went into the bedroom to get our dirty clothes. Two hours later, I noticed the washer had gone through the whole cycle with no clothes in it. I told my husband I had run the "cleaning cycle."

I'm always getting up to go get something in the house, and when I get there I can't remember what I came for. I've found my dishwasher detergent in the refrigerator, my car keys in the silverware drawer, and the milk carton sitting in the cupboard beside the plates.

I got in a tizzy about my mental state and how ditzy I was going to be after all the chemotherapy drugs went through my system. I had to pay more attention to details. I learned to make lists. I asked friends to remind me of activities and help me remember stuff. I also decided that after all the dumb things I had already done, nobody would notice the change!

I praise You, Lord, for Your love is not based on what I do but on what You have already done. You came to this earth because of Your matchless love. You were born in a manger and died on a cross paying for my sin. No one has ever poured out that much love for me.

Lord, I am grateful it is not up to me in this life. You are the Master Builder. Even when I cannot see it, You have a blueprint that is perfect, lacking in nothing. You graciously remind me that You are in control and Your plan is best.

I fall on my knees before You, Lord. Accept my offering this day of praise and adoration for Your gift of love in my life—the love that allows me to fail and be forgiven, the love that allows me to laugh at myself. Even when there are tough things, You always bring joy because You have clothed me with the garment of salvation. You have claimed me as Your own. I praise You, God, for Your gifts this day.

Lois Olmstead
Author, *Breast Cancer and Me*

TODAY'S TIP: Keep your sense of humor when you do ditzy things!

PRAYER REFERENCE: Isaiah 61:10

Faith, Suffering, Endurance, Character, Hope!

*May the God who gives endurance and
encouragement give you a spirit of unity . . . so
that with one heart and mouth you may glorify
the God and Father of our Lord Jesus Christ.*

—ROMANS 15:5–6

Little did I know that my surgery to remove a benign tumor would become a six-hour ordeal! A cancerous thyroid and twenty-four malignant lymph nodes were removed from my neck. In an instant, my family entered the cancer world with the same jolt that hits all who have been diagnosed.

The fears experienced seem larger than life. Chemotherapy, radiation, and the thought of death flooded my mind during those initial days. Slowly, through the struggle, God began to produce an endurance I had not known. I was bolstered by the enormous amount of love and prayers received from family, close friends, and our community.

Years later, God clearly led us to begin a cancer ministry, which I lead today. This organization has trained more than eight hundred cancer survivors to go into the world as beacons of hope for newly diagnosed patients. God used this difficult time in my life to build endurance and character in me —and to give hope to many others going through the same experience. What great things might He have in store for you?

Almighty God, I rejoice in the hope of Your glory. Not only so, but I also rejoice in my sufferings, because I know that You have promised that suffering produces perseverance; perseverance, character; and character, hope. And hope does not disappoint, because You poured out Your love into my heart by the Holy Spirit, whom You gave to me. Continue to increase Your presence within, that I may grow in perseverance and character and be a light to others who need to experience Your hope.

You are the Light of the world. I have seen Your glory, the glory of the One and Only, who came from the Father, full of grace and truth. And through Your Spirit, You have made me a light in the world. Help me to shine brightly before others, that they may see my good deeds (empowered by You!) and praise You, my Father in heaven.

Nancy Tucker
President, CanCare

TODAY'S TIP: Consider the positive by-products of cancer.

PRAYER REFERENCES: Romans 5:2–5; Romans 15:5–6; John 1:5, 14; Matthew 5:14, 16

So Much More

*Now to Him who is able to do
exceedingly abundantly above all
that we ask or think, according
to the power that works in us.*
—Ephesians 3:20 NKJV

I tend to try to solve all my problems. But this time I could not figure out how we were going to pay for the $40,000 bill from my bone marrow transplant. People had already given us so much. The hospital said we could pay what we could every month. I figured that at a youth pastor's salary, that would be about $25 a month over the next hundred years!

So I stressed about it until one day I finally gave it over to God. I said, "Lord, You have taken care of me so far. This financial situation is Yours. I cannot do this anymore." As I wrote this in my journal, I felt a tremendous weight fall off of my shoulders.

The next day as I opened the mail, I noticed an envelope from the hospital. Thinking it was the same bill, I carelessly opened it. To my surprise, it was a letter explaining that the hospital had written off the total amount of our bill. Tears streamed down my face as I realized how much God can do for us.

Thank You, Jesus, for saying, "Come to me, all you who are weary and burdened, and I will give you rest." How grateful I am that You lift my burdens off me and give me rest.

Forgive me for holding on to my burdens too tightly and trying to figure them out myself. Help me be like King Hezekiah, who took his problem and laid it out before You. I join him in praying, "O LORD, God of Israel, enthroned between the cherubim, you alone are God over all the kingdoms of the earth. You have made heaven and earth. Give ear, O LORD, and hear; open your eyes, O LORD, and see." [Just as Hezekiah then shared his problem, share your greatest burdens with the Lord.]

Thank You for wanting me to turn to You first and for working in ways beyond my scope of understanding. You are able to do immeasurably more than anything I can ask or imagine!

Trina Mavin

Pastor's wife and homemaker

Today's Tip: If you have been holding on to something too tightly and trying to figure it out yourself, take a moment to release your cares to God.

Prayer References: Matthew 11:28; 2 Kings 19:15–16; Ephesians 3:20

When Faith Falters

I do believe, but help me not to doubt!
—MARK 9:24 NLT

I was stumbling in my faith. Hadn't two medical doctors said the recurrence of breast cancer in my lung was fatal? Hadn't my husband and I heard that surgery and treatment could only give me a little more time? I didn't want "a little more time." Our two young children were adopted and had already experienced devastating trauma in their lives. They desperately needed me. But how could I doubt the knowledge of such learned doctors? I groaned in nonsensical misery as I prayed and asked God to remember these precious ones with his mercy.

One Sunday morning, a young friend slipped a note card to me. It read, "Dear Eva, 'With long life will I satisfy her and show her my salvation' (Psalm 91:16)." This note was decorated with flowers cut from a seed catalog. During their early years of marriage, my friend and her husband had very little of this world's wealth, but she practiced a mighty faith, which she shared with me.

It's been eighteen years since that time. I still carry that card in my Bible as a reminder that our Lord is not limited by human understanding!

Father God, thank You for giving me friends who pray in faith, believing You hear and will answer their prayers. They know You as the Great Physician—and so do I. Thank You for those who hold on to faith when my thinking cannot be trusted because of the effects of my treatments.

I sense the strength and comfort from these precious petitions that ascend to You. I am so grateful Your eyes watch over those who do right and Your ears are open to their prayers. I also thank You for Your Holy Spirit, who works in my spirit and who even prays for me with groans that cannot be expressed in words.

As the man said to Jesus, "I do believe; help me overcome my unbelief!" I ask that You also help me and my unbelief. Help me remember that whenever my faith falters, I can rest knowing that nothing is too difficult for You. With You, all things are possible!

Eva Rice
Retired office worker and former public speaker

TODAY'S TIP: Enlist a friend or two to be prayer buddies for you.

PRAYER REFERENCES: Matthew 21:22; 1 Peter 3:12; Romans 8:26; Mark 9:24; Jeremiah 32:17; Matthew 19:26

Unexpectedly Lonely

My flesh and my heart may fail,
but God is the strength of
my heart and my portion forever.
—Psalm 73:26

When you're in the middle of a major illness, you think, *When I get well, my life will be normal again.* You think "normal" will happen automatically when your health is restored. But there's an emotional transition between sick and well, and it doesn't come with a road map or an instruction sheet.

When my treatment ended and the doctor said I was in full remission, I found myself in totally new territory. Expecting to feel happy and full of joy, instead I found myself tense—and *lonely*. Now that was an emotion I hadn't expected! But that's truly how I felt. Despite all my complaining about the ongoing tests and medications, when the oncologist announced that I would need only regular MRIs but not weekly appointments, it felt as though I were being tossed out on my own.

It took hard work, plenty of prayer, and help from my doctors and friends to reset my attitude. Today I'm determined to see remission as a time of rebirth—a time of new life and hope. Now I'm a pioneer exploring new territory in this extended life God has given me.[20]

You are the strength of my heart and my portion forever. I am grateful You walk with me and when the road gets tough, carry me. Through all life brings, I desire to put my hope in You, my Savior and my God!

I am grateful that when trials threaten to overwhelm me, You have given me the ability to choose another way—Your way of boundless love, joy, and grace. It is so easy, in the midst of painful times, to want to withdraw from life, shut the door, and turn off the phone. But that's the wrong thing to do—in so many ways. I confess that by shutting others out, I allow myself to be consumed by the problem. I fail to share in the blessings that may come to them and to me as You work in all our lives.[21]

Barbara Johnson
Best-selling author, *Plant a Geranium in Your Cranium*

TODAY'S TIP: No one can go back and make a brand-new start, but anyone can start *now* and make a brand-new ending.

PRAYER REFERENCE: Psalm 73:26

A New Normal

But we all, with unveiled face,
beholding as in a mirror the glory of
the Lord, are being transformed into
the same image from glory to glory.

—2 CORINTHIANS 3:18 NKJV

Normal is relative, is it not? It is normal to open an umbrella on a rainy day but rather odd to carry one on a sunny day. It is quite normal to laugh at a good joke but incredibly poor taste to laugh while someone is crying.

The "normals" of life vary with the changes of life. A new job, a new home, marriage, and children are life changes that require adjustment. Cancer led me into a new normal that would forever remain. It began when my doctor said, "We can't save the breast." She had made two attempts to remove my cancer, and each surgery revealed there was more left behind. Her wisdom and experience concluded that the breast must be removed, and so it was.

My reflection in the mirror and the way I dressed every day would be vastly unlike what it had been thus far in my life. Losing my breast took me through the normal grieving process. Once I accepted my new "normal," I was able to embrace the new me!

Father, thank You for shaping me and making me into the person You want me to be. All the changes in my life have been granted by Your loving hand and supplied with Your grace. I am grateful that my outward appearance is not all that has changed. You are transforming me on the inside, as well. This transformation is sometimes painful, but thankfully, You are the only One who sees it. Thank You for transforming me day by day according to Your perfect plan, into the image of Your Son. I am so grateful that You, who began a good work in me, will carry it on to completion!

Almighty God, may it be normal that when I face change, I seek Your face. I want to run to You, not away from You. You are my strength every morning, and You help me in times of distress. You long to be gracious to me. You rise to show me compassion. Blessed are those who wait for You!

Patti Nagle
Homemaker

TODAY'S TIP: Take a friend and visit a breast cancer boutique that sells bathing suits and bras. You will be surprised at how beautiful your new normal can be!

PRAYER REFERENCES: 2 Corinthians 3:18; Philippians 1:6; Isaiah 33:2; Isaiah 30:18

Renewing Your Mind

*Do not conform any longer to the
pattern of this world, but be transformed
by the renewing of your mind.*

—ROMANS 12:2

My friend Jeff was a constant source of inspiration to me as we went through cancer together. Doctors found and removed a rapidly growing form of brain cancer in his skull. But within a year, the cancer returned in his brain, beyond the reaches of radiation and chemotherapy. Jeff left behind a beautiful wife and four daughters, ages two to sixteen.

Amazingly, Jeff always had a smile on his face and was filled with tremendous joy. When I was undergoing chemotherapy, he would ask my husband, Gordy, about me often. His selflessness blew us away. Truly, this was the transforming of a mind that easily could have said, "This is unfair, God!" Jeff was totally committed to serving God, encouraging others, and doing His will despite what cancer was doing to his body.

God would bring others into my life who would show me how to live, even in the darkest moments, but Jeff had a profound impact on my life.

Thank You, Lord, for real people like King David, who cried out as I have, "How long must I wrestle with my thoughts and every day have sorrow in my heart?" And yet, only a few verses later, You had completely renewed David's mind, and he was able to proclaim, "But I trust in Your unfailing love; my heart rejoices in Your salvation. I will sing to the LORD, for he has been good to me." Thank You for all the ways You have shown Your goodness to me.

I am so grateful for people who show me how to live each day, cancer patients who have mentored and ministered to me. Thank you for men and women who have served You with their whole being even though they were suffering physically.

I thank You that You desire to renew my mind, to restore me when I'm down. You are gracious to help me. Thank You for helping me to be salt and light to others going through difficult circumstances. How I desire to show others the way to You by being a godly testimony of Your love.

Laura Geist

TODAY'S TIP: Try to encourage someone going through a personal struggle. You will be blessed too.

PRAYER REFERENCES: Psalm 13:2, 5, 6; Romans 12:2; Matthew 5:13–14

Hope

*You will be secure, because there is hope; you
will look about you and take your rest in safety.
You will lie down, with no one to make you
afraid, and many will court your favor.*

—JOB 11:18–19

One thing I realized after my bout with uterine cancer is
that it became very important for me to hear the words "cancer survivor." As my ten-year anniversary of survivorship
quickly approaches, I am here to tell you that every day I
praise God for bringing me not only through the cancer but
through these past ten years of *living*.

I praise Him that He performed the miracle of creating me,
healing me, and allowing me to experience *hope*—hope in Him
and through Him. He did this by placing other cancer survivors in my path. How those survivors ministered to me!
They were still *living* as walking, talking, breathing individuals.
This filled my heart with hope.

I encourage all cancer survivors never to keep quiet but to let
others know not only about the cancer but, most importantly,
about the Author of hope. To Him be the glory.

Hope

I praise You, Lord, for Your eyes are on those who fear You, on those whose hope is in Your unfailing love. You are able to deliver me from death and keep me alive and hopeful in difficult times. I am so grateful I can rest in You because You have promised to help and protect me. In You my heart rejoices, for I trust in Your holy name. May Your unfailing love rest upon me, Lord, even as I put my hope in You.

Thank You for how this cancer has forced me to place my hope and trust in You. I am experiencing Your healing strength and Your comforting arms around me. Thank You for the cancer survivors You have placed in my life who have given me such hope. You are a personal God, who is in the details of our lives. I praise You for who You are and for the hope that is born of You through Your Son, Jesus, in whose name I pray. Praise You, God of hope.

Julie Duesing
Homemaker and sales manager

TODAY'S TIP: Begin a journal of your cancer journey now. Later you will have the privilege of looking back and remembering how the God of hope showed Himself faithful.

PRAYER REFERENCE: Psalm 33:18–22

Is Jesus Enough?

*I once thought all these things were so
very important, but now I consider them
worthless because of what Christ has done.*

—PHILIPPIANS 3:7 NLT

My cancer diagnosis was especially upsetting to my husband. He had lost his first wife twenty years earlier to Lou Gehrig's disease when they were still newlyweds. To watch me face an uncertain future was more than he felt he could bear.

One day he came upon a car with a bumper sticker that read, "Jesus is enough." He was so overcome with worry and fear of losing yet another wife that he wondered out loud, "Is He really?"

Have you asked that same question?

If I lose a breast, is Jesus enough?

If I lose my hair to chemo, is Jesus enough?

If I have to quit work, is Jesus enough?

And worst of all, if the cancer doesn't get cured, is Jesus really enough?

My husband answered that question two weeks later when he preached a powerful sermon entitled "Jesus Is Enough." In it, he reminded all of us that God doesn't *need* to do another thing for us on this earth. He has given us His one and only Son, and in Him we have everything we need to cope with this life and every promise for eternal life. Jesus is enough!

Lord, help me to feel in my heart what I know in my head—that You can and will meet every need I have during this cancer journey. Help me deal with the changes this disease is bringing into my life. I pray that they will be temporary ones and that my health will be restored completely. But even if it's not, help my soul to be satisfied in You alone.

It feels unfair to have cancer after I've tried so hard to live for You. And then I remember that You lived completely for Your Father, and life still was very unfair to You. I'm glad You understand what I'm feeling and facing. I am so grateful that You, an all powerful God, have given me everything I need for this life. Thank You for this very great and precious promise. I praise You for being all I need—for being enough!

Lynn Eib
Author, *When God and Cancer Meet,*
Finding the Light in Cancer's Shadow

☞ TODAY'S TIP: Listen for the word *enough* in conversations, and when you hear it, remind yourself that Jesus is enough.

☞ PRAYER REFERENCES: 2 Peter 1:3–4; Psalm 42:1

Passing Through Baca

Blessed is the man whose strength is in You,
whose heart is set on pilgrimage. As they pass
through the Valley of Baca, they make it a spring.
—PSALM 84:5–6 NKJV

On their way to worship God in Jerusalem, Jewish pilgrims had to pass through the Valley of Baca, literally the "Valley of Tears." This valley was a parched and arid pass filled with thorns, wild animals, and roving bandits. Not a place for your next family vacation!

As we travel along life's journey to meet our Savior in heaven, God may ask us to travel through our own Baca. This "Valley of Tears" may include our cancer journey with its endless doctor appointments, malignant test results, and painful procedures.

But like the Jewish pilgrims who found the wells dug among Baca's scorched landscape, we will find God's springs of refreshment in our desert if we turn to Him. These valley experiences strip away our self-sufficiency and bring us to the realization that Jesus is all we need. Only our Savior is able to guide us through the perils of Baca to Zion's glory.

Lord, thank You for walking beside me in the valleys of my life and leading me to the cool, refreshing well of Your goodness. Allow these Baca experiences to deepen my trust in You. You have told me that Your grace is sufficient and Your strength is made perfect in my weakness. Empty me of all of my own strength so that I may rely on Your might. I praise You for Your promise that I go from strength to strength till I appear before You in Zion. It is amazing to consider that with You I don't go from strength to weakness but only from strength to strength because it is Your strength at work in me.

I am grateful for the joy and springs of refreshment I am able to experience in the midst of the trials. You promise that when the way is rough, my patience has a chance to grow. And when it is in full bloom, I will be strong in character, full, and complete.

As I walk through the valley of the shadow of death, I will fear no evil. Lord, You are with me. Surely, goodness and mercy will follow me all the days of my life.

Laura Geist

⟋ TODAY'S TIP: When the cancer journey feels like a dry valley of life, reflect on the springs of refreshment that God has given along the way and thank Him for them.

⟋ PRAYER REFERENCES: 2 Corinthians 12:9; Psalm 84:7; James 1:2–4; Psalm 23:4, 6

A Final Word

Throughout the pages of this book, you have read some amazing stories of God's faithfulness to women who have journeyed through cancer. We hope that you have laughed, cried, and been inspired by their stories and by the prayers that followed. For these women, cancer was a comma, not a period, in the sentences of their lives. Why? Because these women had put their faith in God's Son, Jesus Christ, and invited Him into their hearts as their personal Lord and Savior.

They had already seen God working in their lives, answering their prayers and encouraging them through life's trials. Their cancer experience was a huge challenge but also an opportunity for them to draw closer to Jesus, who Himself was well acquainted with pain and suffering (Hebrews 2:18). Because of their trust in Him, Jesus turned their anxiety into unexpected joy and their pain into an opportunity to serve Him. Through prayer and praise to their Creator—even through cancer, their hearts were set free from the fear of the unknown.

GOD'S PLAN FOR RELATIONSHIP

Friend, where are you on this journey? Have you personally asked Jesus Christ to come into your life? We know that not everyone suffers from cancer. But everyone suffers from a "disease" called sin, which is simply disobeying God in any manner. Romans 3:23 says, "All have sinned and fall short of the glory of God." This disobedience separates us from a perfect, holy God.

We can never earn our way into God's favor with human efforts, like good works, giving money, or even attending church. Romans 6:23 says, "The wages of sin is death, but the gift of God is eternal life in Christ Jesus our Lord." God has provided a cure for this sin "disease"! His name is Jesus Christ.

God Himself, in the form of His Son, Jesus, came to earth more than two thousand years ago to show us what He was like. He lived a perfect life, loved and healed sick people, and then suffered a cruel death on a Roman cross for our sake. Romans 5:8 says, "While we were still sinners, Christ died for us." His death provided the only remedy for man's sin. Jesus said, "I am the way and the truth and the life. No one comes to the Father except through me" (John 14:6). He made this bold claim and then proved it was true by His resurrection from the dead.

God offers us the free gift of eternal life if we receive Him and turn from our sinful condition. "To all who received him, to those who believed in his name, he gave the right to become children of God" (John 1:12). The women in this book could be joyful during their cancer journey because they knew where their life's journey would ultimately end, from cancer or otherwise—in eternity with Jesus!

We know you have made many important decisions as a cancer patient. But choosing to ask Jesus into your heart is the most important decision you'll ever make. It's a life-changing decision because Jesus becomes the center of your life. He will give your life peace, joy, and purpose like you have never known before. It is also a future-changing decision because asking Christ into your life means you will spend eternity with God.

If you would like to receive Christ today, you can pray this simple prayer:

> *Jesus, I accept You into my life to be my personal Lord and Savior. I confess that I am a sinner, and I know that You died and rose again so that my sins might be forgiven and that I might have eternal life with You. I turn from my sin and give my life to You. Please come into my heart and help me to lead a life pleasing to You. Amen.*

We rejoice with you if you made this important decision to ask Christ into your heart! We want to assure you that the moment you received Christ by faith, several things happened. First and foremost, Jesus came into your life (Revelation 3:20; Colossians 1:27), and your sins were forgiven (Ephesians 1:7).

You also became a child of God (John 1:12). Because you are now His child, you have begun a wonderful journey with God in this life (John 10:10; 2 Corinthians 5:17; Ephesians 2:10) and will spend eternity with Him in heaven when this life is over (John 5:24; John 14:2).[22]

True Healing

You've heard from many cancer survivors in this book. We rejoice in God's plan to give them more years of service on this earth. We also want to recognize the fact that many women have been healed in a different way. They have entered their eternal home with God. The only true, lasting healing is through this personal relationship with God through Jesus Christ. We all will die, whether now or later. Though we hope for later, God desires that we come to a place where we desire Him whether we are here with Him or in heaven. In essence, life is not about the length of time on this earth but where we are with our Creator.

We know there are many stories of women who have persevered through cancer and have entered their heavenly home. One such woman was Brenda Borne. Her friends—Grace Gladden, Suzanne Tucker, and Suzie Bell—shared Brenda's story with us. It is a story of triumph over death!

Grace was the first to know Brenda. She felt God nudging

her to invite Brenda to a Bible study. When Brenda joined the Bible study, she was not really sure why she was there. She only knew that she was seeking something; and when Grace invited her, it sounded like something she wanted to try. She considered herself spiritual but readily told the group, "God I know. Jesus I am not so sure about."

Later that year, Brenda was diagnosed with leukemia, and the amazing journey began. As Brenda continued with treatment, she continued to study. When she was too sick to attend the weekly sessions, her three friends brought the lessons to her. They gathered at her house and tried to answer her numerous questions. Often they carried the study to the hospital room as she went in and out several times. Brenda was an eager student and hungrily devoured God's Word. Before she entered the hospital for the last time, she was witnessing to other cancer patients.

Having always known of God's presence and power, she discovered the God of relationship through Jesus Christ. She professed to others, "You can believe and adhere to all these other religions, all these other men who profess to know the way, but there is only one of them who was willing to die for you."

As Brenda battled with cancer, she embraced it as an opportunity to grow in her new relationship with the One who had paid the ultimate price for her life. God had supplied Brenda with all that she needed for the road ahead. Her spiritual understanding of Him grew rapidly as she daily surrendered her life to His eternal purpose and glory. Brenda viewed her physical sufferings as an offering to Christ and allowed it to be a witness to the world. Her ultimate witness was one of acceptance and joy as she accepted the reality of her disease. Her death left a lasting impact on her friends and in her community. It still does. Her friends were her cord of three strands, stronger than any of them could be alone.

The key to contentment is keeping our eyes on eternity and not on the trials. We have the privilege of walking with our Lord each step of the way. Let's do it with joy and freedom, knowing that every detail of our lives is in God's loving and faithful care.

WE'D LOVE TO HEAR FROM YOU

We'd love to hear your story. Please let us know if this book has been a help to you in your spiritual journey by contacting us through our Web site, www.prayingthroughcancer.com.

God bless you!

Notes

1. Charles R. Swindoll, *Elijah: A Man of Heroism and Humility* (Nashville: W Publishing Group, 2000).

2. Adapted from Pat Palau, "Is There a Christian Response to Cancer?" *Moody Magazine* (October 1981), 25.

3. C. S. Lewis, *The Problem of Pain* (New York: MacMillan, 1962), 93.

4. Adapted from Barbara Johnson, *Plant a Geranium in Your Cranium* (Nashville: W Publishing Group, 2002), 20.

5. Hannah Whitall Smith, *The Christian's Secret of a Happy Life* (New York: Ballantine Books, 1942, repr. 1970), 190.

6. Author unknown. Found in Mary Prentiss Smith, "Lean Hard"

7. Randy Travis, "Forever and Ever, Amen". Words and Music by Paul Overstreet and Don Schlitz. © 1987 Screen Gems-EMI Music Inc., Scarlet Moon Music, Universal Music Corp. and Don Schlitz Music. All rights for Don Schlitz Music controlled and administered by Universal Music Corp. All rights reserved. International copyright secured. Used by Permission.

8. Mrs. Charles E. Cowman, *Streams in the Desert* (Uhrichsville, Ohio: Barbour, 1965), October 12 entry.

9. Adapted from Barbara Johnson, *Plant a Geranium in Your Cranium*, 15–16.

10. Ibid., 151.

11. Lois Olmstead, *Breast Cancer and Me* (Camp Hill, Pa.: Christian Publications, 1996). Reprinted with permission.

12. Adapted from Barbara Johnson, *Plant a Geranium in Your Cranium*, 54.

13. Ibid., 76.

14. Elisabeth Elliot, *A Path Through Suffering: Discovering the Relationship Between God's Mercy and Our Pain* (Ann Arbor, Mich.: Servant, 1990), 69.

15. Jurjen Beumer, *Henri Nouwen: A Restless Seeking for God* (New York: Crossroad, 1997), 85.

16. Adapted from Barbara Johnson, *Plant a Geranium in Your Cranium*, 6–7.

17. Ibid., 9

18. Lois Olmstead, *Breast Cancer and Me*. Reprinted with permission.

19. Corrie Ten Boom, as quoted on www.maxlucado.com/read/in.the.word/index5.html. Accessed May 9, 2005.

20. Adapted from Barbara Johnson, *Plant a Geranium in Your Cranium*, 137–138.

21. Ibid., 138.

22. Adapted from *Four Spiritual Laws*, Campus Crusade for Christ.